Living Together:

Why Israel And Palestine Must Find A Way Forward

Alexandre-luc Wahlström Smith

Naive

Contents

The History of the Conflict and the
Need for a New Approach

It is essential to delve even deeper into the rich history of the Israeli-Palestinian conflict to truly understand its complexities. The roots of this conflict can be traced back to the late 19th century when waves of Jewish immigration to Palestine increased due to rising antisemitism in Europe and the Zionist movement advocating for a Jewish homeland.

In the late 1800s, as Jewish communities faced persecution and discrimination in various parts of Europe, the Zionist movement emerged as a response, promoting the idea of a Jewish homeland in Palestine. Influenced by nationalist and colonial ideas of the time, Zionist leaders sought to establish a haven for Jewish people, a place where they could assert their national identity and live in safety.

The First Zionist Congress, held in Basel, Switzerland, in 1897, marked a significant milestone for the movement. Theodor Herzl, considered the father of modern political Zionism, convened the congress, bringing together diverse Jewish voices from across the world to discuss the establishment of a Jewish state in Palestine. Although the Zionist movement faced opposition from some Jewish communities who were skeptical of political Zionism, the momentum towards a Jewish homeland continued to grow.

As Jewish immigration to Palestine increased, tensions

naturally arose with the Arab population living in the region. These tensions centered around competing claims to the land, access to resources, and the aspirations of two peoples with deep historical and cultural connections to the territory. These conflicting national narratives and territorial claims have been at the heart of the Israeli-Palestinian conflict ever since.

The British Empire's involvement further complicated the situation. After the defeat of the Ottoman Empire in World War I, the League of Nations granted Britain a mandate over Palestine. In the Balfour Declaration of 1917, the British government expressed support for the establishment of a "national home for the Jewish people" while also stating that "nothing shall be done which may prejudice the civil and religious rights of existing non Jewish communities in Palestine."
This declaration set the stage for further Jewish immigration to Palestine, leading to demographic shifts and land disputes between Jewish settlers and Arab communities. As tensions escalated, various clashes and instances of violence occurred throughout the mandate period.

In 1947, the United Nations proposed a partition plan for Palestine, known as UN Resolution 181, recommending the creation of separate Jewish and Arab states and an international administration for Jerusalem. The plan was accepted by Jewish leaders but rejected by Arab leaders, who saw it as an infringement on their rights and an unjust partition of land. This rejection led to the outbreak of violence and the first Arab-Israeli war in 1948.

Following the declaration of Israel's independence in 1948, neighboring Arab countries, including Egypt, Jordan, Syria, and Iraq, launched a military intervention against the newly formed state. The ensuing Arab-Israeli war resulted in a victory for Israel, while also leading to the displacement of hundreds of thousands of Palestinians, who became refugees in the conflict.

This refugee crisis deepened the sense of injustice and dispossession among Palestinians, fueling a lasting grievance and a demand for the right of return to their ancestral lands. Throughout subsequent decades, the Israeli-Palestinian conflict has been defined by the ongoing struggle over territory, self-determination, and recognition of historical narratives.

Moreover, the conflict has become intertwined with religious and cultural identities. The land of historic Palestine holds great religious significance for Jews, Christians, and Muslims, with sites such as the Western Wall, the Church of the Holy Sepulchre, and the Al-Aqsa Mosque conjuring deep emotions and spiritual connections. The overlapping claims to these holy sites have regularly sparked tensions and escalations of violence.

Political leadership on both sides has also played a pivotal role in perpetuating the conflict. While some leaders have pursued peace negotiations and made concessions, progress has often been hindered by domestic political pressures, wavering commitment, and a lack of trust. The complexities of the issues at stake, combined with political calculations, have made finding common ground and reaching a sustainable agreement elusive.

Efforts to resolve the conflict have seen both success and failure. The Oslo Accords of the 1990s, for example, provided a framework for negotiations, but their implementation faced significant challenges, and the intended final status agreement was never reached. Other initiatives, such as the Camp David Summit in 2000 and the Annapolis Conference in 2007, also failed to produce lasting peace.

The current state of affairs is marked by sporadic outbreaks of violence, ongoing settlement expansion, and severe security concerns for both Israelis and Palestinians. The cycle of violence and retaliation has resulted in a deepening of mutual mistrust, fear, and hostility, further complicating the path to peace.

Given these persistent challenges, there is an urgent need for a new approach to resolve the Israeli-Palestinian conflict. The traditional methods of conflict resolution and diplomacy have proven insufficient thus far. It is crucial to explore fresh ideas and perspectives that can break the cycle of violence and offer a sustainable path towards coexistence and peace.

In the subsequent chapters, we will continue to delve into the complexity of the Israeli Palestinian conflict. We will examine the narratives, grievances, and aspirations from both the Israeli and Palestinian perspectives. We will also explore the challenges to peace, such as the issues of borders, settlements, Jerusalem, and the right of return for Palestinian refugees. Additionally, we will consider practical solutions for coexistence and peaceful cohabitation, the role of the international community and the United Nations, regional actors, and the potential benefits of coexistence to create a comprehensive understanding of the conflict and inspire new approaches to its resolution.

Living Together: Why Israel And Palestine
Must Find A Way Forward

———

The Origins of the Israeli-Palestinian Conflict

The Israeli-Palestinian conflict is a deeply rooted and complex issue that has spanned over a century, with multiple layers of historical, political, and cultural factors shaping its origins. Understanding the intricacies of this conflict requires delving into a wider range of events and influences that contributed to the ongoing struggle between Jews and Arabs for control over the same land.

The roots of this conflict can be traced back to the late 19th century, a time when the notion of nationhood was gaining traction worldwide. In Palestine, a region under Ottoman rule with a predominantly Arab population, a sense of Arab nationalism began to emerge. Meanwhile, as anti-Semitism grew in Europe, the Zionist movement took root, advocating for the establishment of a Jewish homeland. Theodor Herzl, considered the father of modern political Zionism, called for the creation of a Jewish state where Jews could find refuge and self-determination.

The early Zionist pioneers faced several challenges in their quest for a homeland. Alongside the local Arab population's opposition to Jewish immigration, Arab nationalist movements were also gaining momentum in the region. The presence of Jews seeking to establish a national home in Palestine, a land they considered their ancestral home, invoked feelings of apprehension among the local Arab population. For the Arabs, who considered themselves the indigenous inhabitants of Palestine, the influx of

Jewish immigrants threatened their demographic majority and their aspiration for self-rule.

Geopolitical developments further complicated the situation. During World War I, the weakening of the Ottoman Empire and the rise of Arab nationalism prompted Arab leaders to ally themselves with the British against the Ottomans. In the midst of these alliances, British officials issued the Balfour Declaration in 1917, expressing support for "the establishment in Palestine of a national home for the Jewish people." The declaration, while significant for Jewish aspirations, reneged on the earlier promises made to Arabs for independence.

After the war, Britain was granted a mandate to administer Palestine from the League of Nations. Their administration faced numerous challenges in reconciling the conflicting demands of Jews and Arabs. Zionist immigrants continued to arrive, purchasing land and establishing Jewish settlements, contributing to increased tensions with the Arab population. Arab protests and resistance grew, and British forces found themselves trying to maintain control amidst the escalating violence.

Arab strategic objectives shifted during World War II. Fearing the continuance of British hegemony in the region, Arab leaders attempted to align themselves with the Axis powers. As a result, they lost international sympathy and placed their aspirations for Palestinian independence on the backburner during the war. Meanwhile, the horrors of the Holocaust intensified global sympathy for the Zionist cause and heightened the urgency to find a solution for Jewish refugees.

In 1947, the United Nations proposed a partition plan for Palestine, which would have divided the land into separate Jewish and Arab states. The plan was accepted by Jewish leaders but vehemently rejected by Arab representatives, who perceived the partition as an infringement on their rights and an abandonment of their aspirations for a unified Palestine. Arab neighbors threatened military intervention if the plan were implemented, while Jewish leaders saw the partition as a necessary step toward establishing a Jewish state.

The declaration of the State of Israel in May 1948 triggered the first Arab-Israeli war. Arab states, determined to prevent the creation of a Jewish state, launched a military campaign against Israel. This war resulted in the displacement of hundreds of thousands of Palestinian Arabs, contributing to what is now known as the Palestinian refugee crisis. At the same time, Israel emerged victorious, solidifying its presence in the region.

The aftermath of the war marked a significant turning point in the conflict. The displacement of Palestinians and the establishment of an independent Jewish state created a deeply entrenched divide, with narratives of dispossession and victimhood taking shape on both sides. Arab nations, feeling betrayed by the international community and embittered by their military defeat, refused to recognize Israel's legitimacy, further fueling the conflict and leading to subsequent rounds of violence and hostilities.

Over the years, the conflict has become increasingly complicated, with territorial disputes, access to resources, and the status of Jerusalem adding further layers of complexity. Peace negotiations, including the Oslo Accords in the 1990s, have faced numerous setbacks, with issues such as the expansion of Israeli settlements, security concerns, and the division of land remaining major points of contention.

Acknowledging the multifaceted nature of the conflict is essential when seeking a solution. Recognizing the historical grievances, addressing the aspirations of both Israelis and Palestinians for self-determination, and engaging in meaningful dialogue are crucial steps towards fostering understanding and building a foundation for a just and lasting peace in the region. However, finding a comprehensive resolution remains a daunting task that requires the commitment of both parties, as well as the international community, to overcome the barriers that have hindered a peaceful resolution for far too long.

Living Together: Why Israel And Palestine
Must Find A Way Forward

———

Colonialism and its Impact on the Conflict

Throughout history, colonialism has played a significant role in shaping conflicts around the world, and the Israeli-Palestinian conflict is no exception. The impact of colonialism on this protracted conflict cannot be overstated, as it has had lasting effects on the attitudes, perceptions, and power dynamics between Israelis and Palestinians.

Colonialism in the region dates back to the late 19th century when various European powers began to exert their influence in the Middle East. This period of imperial expansion was driven by a combination of economic, strategic, and ideological motives. European powers saw the Middle East as a valuable area for trade, resources, and geopolitical control. They also held a sense of racial superiority, believing they had a civilizing mission to bring progress and enlightenment to the indigenous peoples of the region.

The Ottoman Empire, which controlled Palestine at the time, was crumbling, and this power vacuum allowed for European powers, particularly Britain, to increase their involvement in the region. The British, driven by their imperial ambitions and strategic interests, saw an opportunity in the land of Palestine. In 1917, Arthur Balfour, the British Foreign Secretary, issued a public statement known as the Balfour Declaration. This declaration expressed Britain's support for the establishment of a "national home for the Jewish people" in Palestine, which ultimately became a turning point in the Zionist movement.

The Balfour Declaration was not a selfless act but rather an imperialist maneuver by the British. They believed that supporting the Zionist movement would secure their influence in the region and help protect their strategic interests, particularly their access to the Suez Canal. This political decision, made without consulting the indigenous Arab population, set the stage for future conflict.

Under British rule, the population dynamics in Palestine began to shift. Zionist settlers from Europe arrived in larger numbers, acquiring land and establishing Jewish communities, thus fueling the aspirations for a Jewish homeland. The British colonial administration, tasked with managing this complex situation, found themselves struggling to navigate the competing interests of both Jews and Arabs.

Tensions between the two communities gradually escalated, leading to violent clashes and uprisings. The 1920 Nebi Musa riots, 1921 Jaffa riots, and the 1929 Palestine riots were all examples of these escalating tensions. The British, caught in the middle, often resorted to heavy-handed tactics to suppress the violence, further deepening the divide between Jewish and Arab communities.

The impact of colonialism can also be seen in the creation of artificial borders and the partitioning of the land. In 1947, amidst growing tensions and calls for independence, the United Nations proposed a partition plan that would divide Palestine into separate Jewish and Arab states. This plan, known as UN Resolution 181, was met with mixed reactions from both communities.

While the Jewish leadership, represented by the Zionist movement, accepted the proposal, the Arab leadership rejected it. The Arabs viewed the partition plan as an infringement on their rights and an unjust division of their land. Their rejection of the plan led to a series of armed conflicts between Jewish and Arab militias, which further complicated the situation.

The implementation of the partition plan resulted in the displacement of hundreds of thousands of Palestinians, who became refugees in their own land. This mass displacement, known as the Nakba (catastrophe) for Palestinians, further exacerbated tensions between Israelis and Palestinians.

The creation of the state of Israel in 1948 and the subsequent Arab-Israeli wars only deepened these wounds, leaving a legacy of distrust and bitterness that persists to this day. The impact of colonialism on the Israeli-Palestinian conflict extends beyond the historical events leading to the establishment of Israel. It has profoundly influenced the way both Israelis and Palestinians perceive their national identity and their rights to the land.

For Israelis, the Zionist narrative of return to the ancestral homeland holds deep significance. The establishment of Israel, fulfilling the long-awaited dream of statehood for Jews, is seen as a just and necessary response to centuries of persecution and a guarantee of their security in a hostile world. This historical and religious connection to the land is deeply ingrained in the Israeli national psyche, shaping their policies and attitudes towards Palestinians.

On the other hand, Palestinians view themselves as the original inhabitants of the land, dispossessed by colonial powers who were responsible for their displacement and ongoing oppression. They see the establishment of Israel as a direct result of European intervention and a denial of their rights and territorial claims. Palestinians assert their own historical
connection to the land, emphasizing their presence and continuous cultural heritage in the region as evidence of their right to self-determination.

The presence of Jewish settlements in the occupied territories is another legacy of colonialism that perpetuates the conflict. These settlements, built on land claimed by Palestinians for their future state, not only violate international law but also complicate the prospect of a two-state solution. The expansion of settlements displaces Palestinians, fragments their communities, and creates barriers to any potential peace negotiations. The continual expansion of settlements acts as a constant reminder of the power dynamics and asymmetry between Israelis and Palestinians.

In conclusion, colonialism has had a profound and transformative impact on the Israeli Palestinian conflict. From the Balfour Declaration to the creation of Israel and the ongoing presence of settlements, the wounds inflicted by colonial powers continue to shape the perceptions and power dynamics between Israelis and Palestinians. Understanding the historical context of colonialism is crucial for finding a constructive and lasting resolution to this complex and deeply rooted conflict. The echoes of colonialism linger, and addressing these historical injustices will be essential in paving the way for reconciliation and a just and lasting peace.

Living Together: Why Israel And Palestine
Must Find A Way Forward

———

Creation of the State of Israel and the Palestinian Refugee Crisis

The creation of the State of Israel in 1948 was a seminal moment in history that fundamentally transformed the geopolitical landscape of the Middle East. It was the culmination of a long and complex process rooted in the Zionist movement, a 19th-century ideology that sought to establish a homeland for the Jewish people in their ancestral land.

The origins of Zionism can be traced back to the Jewish longing for a return to Zion, as expressed in religious texts and rituals. However, it was in the late 19th century, against the backdrop of growing anti-Semitism in Europe, that the Zionist movement gained traction.

Theodor Herzl, widely regarded as the father of modern political Zionism, published a seminal work in 1896, titled "The Jewish State," which advocated for the establishment of a Jewish homeland in response to the growing persecution and discrimination faced by Jews in Europe.

The Zionist movement gained momentum, with Jews from various parts of the world immigrating to Palestine, eventually leading to increased tensions between Jewish settlers and the indigenous Arab population. The British, who had occupied Palestine under a League of Nations mandate following the collapse of the Ottoman Empire in World War I, struggled to manage the competing aspirations of both groups.

The Balfour Declaration, a letter issued by the British Foreign Secretary in 1917, expressed British support for the establishment of a Jewish homeland in Palestine. This declaration, while viewed by Jews as a significant endorsement, was met with resistance and resentment from the Arab population, who felt betrayed by the British Empire. The British tried to find a balance between their commitment to the Zionist cause and maintaining Arab support in the region, but tensions continued to rise.

In 1947, the United Nations proposed the partition of Palestine into separate Jewish and Arab states, with Jerusalem under international administration. The plan was met with staunch opposition from the Arab states and Palestinian leaders who viewed it as an unjust division of their homeland. They argued that they, too, had a historical and cultural claim to the land.

Amidst this backdrop, on May 14, 1948, David Ben-Gurion, the head of the Jewish Agency, declared the establishment of the State of Israel. Within hours, neighboring Arab states, including Egypt, Jordan, Syria, and Iraq, launched a military intervention to thwart the creation of the Jewish state.

The 1948 war, often referred to as the Arab-Israeli War or War of Independence by Israelis and the Nakba (Arabic for "The Catastrophe") by Palestinians, resulted in a significant displacement of both Jewish and Palestinian communities. Jewish communities in Arab countries also faced violence and expulsion, ultimately leading to their migration to Israel. However, it was the Palestinian experience that defined the refugee crisis. Estimates suggest that approximately 700,000 Palestinians became refugees as a result of the war. Some fled in fear of the fighting, while others were expelled from their homes by Jewish militias.

The mass displacement of Palestinians created a humanitarian crisis that has persisted for decades, with long-lasting consequences for the individuals and their descendants. Palestinian refugees sought refuge in neighboring Arab countries such as Lebanon, Jordan, and Syria, as well as in the West Bank and Gaza Strip, which came under the control of Jordan and Egypt, respectively. They were thrust into a life of uncertainty and hardship, living in makeshift camps with limited access to basic necessities, education, and healthcare.

The Palestinian refugee crisis became one of the most pressing humanitarian issues of the 20th century, and its consequences still reverberate today. The displaced Palestinians and their descendants, now numbering in the millions, continue to struggle for recognition of their right to return to their ancestral homes. The individual stories of loss, resilience, and hope have shaped the collective Palestinian national identity and fuelled the desire for justice.

Efforts to address the Palestinian refugee crisis have been pursued through diplomatic channels, such as the Madrid Conference in 1991 and subsequent negotiations under the Oslo Accords in the 1990s. The issue of the right of return for Palestinian refugees has been a major point of contention, with Israel asserting that accepting all refugees would threaten the Jewish majority of the state.

Proposals for resolving the Palestinian refugee crisis range from options of compensation and financial reparations to allowing a limited number of returnees based on agreed-upon criteria. However, finding a comprehensive solution that satisfies the aspirations and concerns of both Israelis and Palestinians has proven to be an immense challenge.

The Palestinian refugee crisis embodies the complex and deeply rooted issues at the heart of the Israeli-Palestinian conflict. It is not simply a matter of practical resettlement, but also a question of historical, cultural, and political rights. It requires recognition of the immense suffering and displacement experienced by the

Palestinians, as well as an understanding of the concerns and fears of Israelis regarding security and demographics.

Addressing the Palestinian refugee crisis necessitates a solution that upholds principles of justice, human rights, and the right to self-determination for both Israelis and Palestinians. It requires genuine dialogue, empathy, and compromise from all parties involved, as well as the engagement and support of the international community.

Only through a comprehensive and just resolution to the Palestinian refugee crisis can true reconciliation and lasting peace be achieved in the Israeli-Palestinian conflict. The recognition of the rights, dignity, and aspirations of all parties involved is essential for the creation of a future where Israelis and Palestinians can coexist in harmony and prosperity. This requires not only addressing the immediate needs of the refugees but also healing the wounds of the past and fostering conditions for mutual understanding and peaceful coexistence. It demands cooperative efforts, goodwill, and a commitment to breaking the cycle of violence and dispossession.

Efforts to resolve the refugee crisis must also take into account the broader regional context and involve neighboring Arab states. A comprehensive approach that addresses the political, economic, and social dimensions of the Palestinian-Israeli conflict is necessary. This includes addressing the root causes of the conflict, such as the Israeli occupation of Palestinian territories and the ongoing expansion of settlements in the West Bank, which further complicates the issue of Palestinian refugees and their right of return.

International actors, including the United Nations, have a crucial role to play in facilitating dialogue and negotiations between the parties involved. They can provide humanitarian aid and support for the welfare of the refugees, as well as contribute to building the necessary infrastructure and institutions for a future

Palestinian state.

The Palestinian refugee crisis is a deeply human tragedy that has spanned generations. It is a reminder of the consequences of unresolved conflicts and the urgent need for a just and sustainable resolution. The hopes and dreams of millions of Palestinians, as well as Israelis, depend on finding a path towards a future where all can live in peace, security, and dignity. The challenges are immense, but the potential rewards of achieving a just and lasting resolution are immeasurable.

Living Together: Why Israel And Palestine
Must Find A Way Forward

———

Nationalism, Religion, and Identity in the Israeli Palestinian Conflict

Introduction:

The Israeli-Palestinian conflict is a highly intricate and deeply rooted issue, with the dynamics of nationalism, religion, and identity playing significant roles in its perpetuation. These factors have shaped and sustained the narratives, perceptions, and actions of Israelis and Palestinians, further exacerbating the divide between the two communities. Understanding the complexities of nationalism, religion, and identity is critical for comprehending the longstanding nature of the conflict and identifying possible avenues for resolution.

Nationalism:

Nationalism has been a formidable force driving both the Israeli and Palestinian movements for self-determination and sovereignty. For Israelis, the establishment of the State of Israel in 1948 represented the culmination of centuries of Jewish persecution, culminating in the horrors of the Holocaust. The formation of Israel provided a haven and a sense of homeland for Jews worldwide, fulfilling their long-standing national aspirations. However, the realization of the Jewish national dream led to the displacement of nearly 700,000 Palestinians, creating a narrative of dispossession and displacement in the eyes of many Palestinians.

On the other hand, Palestinians view themselves as the indigenous people of the land, tracing their historical roots back to pre-Biblical times. They assert their right to self determination and the establishment of their own state, with East Jerusalem as its capital. The Nakba or "catastrophe" of 1948, marked by the displacement of Palestinians from their homes, created a shared experience of pain, loss, and marginalization, serving as a catalyst for their national struggle. Both communities, driven by their nationalist aspirations, vehemently assert their rightful claim to the land, making territorial compromise a challenging task.

Nationalism, however, has also given rise to extreme ideologies on both sides, leading to a distorted perception of the other and perpetuating a cycle of violence. Radical nationalist ideologies and rhetoric, such as Zionism and Palestinian nationalism, have fueled acts of terrorism, hindered political dialogue, and obstructed efforts for reconciliation. It is crucial to recognize the legitimate national aspirations of both Israelis and Palestinians while promoting moderation, empathy, and a willingness to compromise in order to build mutual understanding and lasting peace.

Religion:

Religion plays a central and complex role in the Israeli-Palestinian conflict, with Judaism and Islam being pivotal to the identities of both communities. The land of Israel/Palestine holds deep religious significance for Jews, Christians, and Muslims alike, further entangling the conflict in religious narratives and aspirations.

For Jews, the land carries immense historical and biblical importance as the ancient homeland promised to them by God. The story of the Exodus, the establishment of the Kingdoms of David and Solomon, and the spiritual fecundity of Jerusalem all contribute to the Jewish connection to the land. Jerusalem, in particular, holds a unique place in Jewish religious tradition, as the site of the First and Second Temples and the spiritual center of Judaism. The Western Wall, the last remnant of the Second Temple, serves as a powerful symbol of Jewish connection to their past and their aspirations for a secure future in the land of Israel.

Similarly, for Muslims, Jerusalem holds great religious significance as the third holiest city after Mecca and Medina. Al-Aqsa Mosque and the Dome of the Rock are revered as sacred sites, preserving the memory of the Prophet Muhammad's Night Journey, during which he is believed to have ascended to heaven. The preservation and protection of these sites are of utmost importance to the Muslim community worldwide, and any negotiations concerning them are highly sensitive.

The intertwining of religious beliefs with nationalist aspirations has amplified the complexity of the conflict. Competing claims to holy sites have fueled tensions and led to clashes between Israelis and Palestinians. Manipulation of religious rhetoric for political gain has further deepened the divide and hindered efforts towards reconciliation. However, it is essential to recognize that religion can also serve as a unifying force, bringing people together and promoting peace. Encouraging interfaith dialogue, educating the youth about the shared historical and cultural heritage of both communities, and facilitating joint religious ceremonies can contribute to building bridges and finding common ground.
Identity:

The Israeli-Palestinian conflict has profoundly shaped the individual and collective identities of Israelis and Palestinians. For Israelis, the struggle for survival and the constant threat of terrorism have reinforced their collective identity as a resilient nation rooted in a historical and biblical connection to the land. The traumas of persecution, culminating in the Holocaust, have further solidified their identity as a people deserving of a homeland, eager to maintain their security and preserve their Jewish heritage.

In contrast, Palestinians have forged an identity characterized by resilience, resistance, and a longing for self-determination. The experiences of displacement, occupation, and everyday struggles have united Palestinians in their quest for justice and freedom. Palestinian identity is deeply woven with a sense of history, culture, and a determination to reclaim their homeland. The Palestinian people are diverse, encompassing Muslims, Christians, and other religious and ethnic groups, all sharing a common narrative of longing for statehood and the right to determine their destiny.

The struggle for identity has often resulted in the dehumanization of the other. Stereotyping, prejudice, and fear have pushed both communities further apart, creating barriers to understanding and empathy. Narratives of victimhood and demonization perpetuate the conflict, making it increasingly challenging to bridge the divide between Israelis and Palestinians. Recognizing and respecting the distinct identities of Israelis and Palestinians while acknowledging the universal values they share as part of the human experience is essential for building trust and promoting peaceful coexistence.

Conclusion:

Nationalism, religion, and identity are deeply intertwined and have played critical roles in perpetuating the Israeli-Palestinian conflict. Understanding these complexities and sensitivities is crucial for finding paths to reconciliation and sustainable peace. By promoting moderate voices, encouraging interfaith dialogue, and fostering a shared sense of humanity, the narrative of the conflict can be transformed. Only then can Israelis and Palestinians build trust, overcome deep-rooted divisions, and work together towards a future of coexistence, mutual respect, and shared prosperity.

Living Together: Why Israel And Palestine
Must Find A Way Forward

———

The Role of Political Leaders in Perpetuating the Conflict

Introduction:

In the complex and deeply rooted Israeli-Palestinian conflict, the role of political leaders cannot be underestimated. Political leaders have not only shaped the course of the conflict but have also perpetuated its longevity. Through their actions, rhetoric, and decisions, leaders on both sides have often prioritized their own political agendas over the pursuit of peace and compromise. This chapter will explore the significant role political leaders have played in perpetuating the Israeli-Palestinian conflict and the challenges this poses to finding a sustainable resolution.

Political Exploitation:

One of the key factors contributing to the perpetuation of the conflict by political leaders is the exploitation of identity politics. By leveraging nationalistic sentiments, leaders have sought to consolidate their power and maintain the support of their respective constituencies. Manipulating historical narratives, leaders have reinforced a sense of collective victimhood and demonized the other side, exacerbating divisions and deepening mistrust. These leaders exploit the fear and insecurity that pervades both Israeli and Palestinian societies, using it to consolidate their support base and maintain a grasp on power.

Obstruction of Peace Processes:

Political leaders on both sides have at times actively obstructed peace processes and negotiations. Through their unwillingness to make significant concessions or compromises, they have impeded progress towards a negotiated settlement. While notable advancements, such as the Oslo Accords in the 1990s, were achieved, subsequent political leaders failed to build upon them. They succumbed to the pressures of hardline factions within their own communities who opposed mutual concessions, leading to a breakdown in trust and renewed hostilities. The reluctance of leaders to prioritize peace over their short term political gains has resulted in repeated missed opportunities for achieving a peaceful resolution.

Use of Violence as a Political Tool:

Tragically, political leaders have also used violence as a means to achieve political objectives, further escalating tensions and perpetuating the cycle of conflict. By resorting to acts of terrorism, military operations, or retaliatory measures, leaders have sought to project strength, assert control, and appease their support base. Suicide bombings, rocket attacks, targeted assassinations, and military offensives have left both Israeli and Palestinian civilians in fear for their lives and have instilled a deep sense of collective trauma. Instead of seeking peaceful resolutions, these leaders have perpetuated cycles of violence and deepened wounds, hindering any potential progress achieved through peace negotiations.

Manipulation of International Support and Aid:

Political leaders have also manipulated international support and aid to their advantage, diverting resources meant for peacebuilding and development towards military purposes or agendas that perpetuate the conflict. Some leaders have used their influence to frame the narrative as one of perpetual victimhood, garnering sympathy and financial support while failing to address the root causes of the conflict. This manipulation of international aid has not only perpetuated the conflict but has hindered socioeconomic progress and perpetuated a culture of dependency. Efforts such as the United Nations Relief and Works Agency for Palestine Refugees (UNRWA) have provided vital assistance but have also become potential tools for political leaders to maintain the status quo rather than seeking substantial, sustainable solutions.

Religion and Political Rhetoric:

Political leaders have invoked religious narratives to galvanize their supporters and legitimize their actions. By intertwining religious beliefs with political rhetoric, leaders have deepened the divide between the Israeli and Palestinian populations. They utilize religion as a powerful tool to foster a sense of identity and mobilize their base, furthering polarization and radicalization. This manipulation of religious sentiment and the portrayal of the conflict as a religious war has perpetuated religious extremism, increasing tensions and preventing the possibility of peaceful coexistence. Leaders on both sides have weaponized faith, using it to further their political agendas rather than promoting understanding and mutual respect between religious communities.

Failure in Leadership and the Path Forward:

The perpetuation of the Israeli-Palestinian conflict by political leaders demonstrates a profound failure in leadership. The prioritization of short-term political gains, the exploitation of fear and insecurity, the obstruction of peace processes, and the manipulation of international support have all contributed to a prolonged and damaging cycle of violence and animosity. To achieve lasting peace, there must be a collective effort to hold leaders accountable for their actions, to promote dialogue and understanding, and to prioritize the well-being of both the Israeli and Palestinian populations over narrow political interests. Genuine and courageous leadership is needed to break the cycle of conflict, foster trust, and pave the way for a peaceful and prosperous future for all. Only through such leadership can the Israeli-Palestinian conflict be resolved and the path to sustainable peace be forged.

Living Together: Why Israel And Palestine Must Find A Way Forward

———

The Current State of Affairs:

Violence, Settlements, and Security

Introduction:

In this chapter, we will delve deeper into the current state of affairs in the Israeli-Palestinian conflict, focusing on the multifaceted issues of violence, settlements, and security. These aspects are key factors perpetuating tensions and pose significant challenges to achieving peaceful coexistence between the two sides.

1. Escalating Violence:

The Israeli-Palestinian conflict has witnessed recurring cycles of violence, leading to immense human suffering and hindering progress towards a solution. Both Israelis and Palestinians have endured the devastating consequences of armed confrontations, including bombings, shootings, and rocket attacks. These acts of violence have claimed countless lives, fostered fear and mistrust, and deepened the divide between the two communities.

Various factors contribute to the escalation of violence, including political grievances, radicalization, and a lack of trust between the parties. Political grievances arise from issues such as the ongoing occupation, the absence of a just and comprehensive resolution, and the failure to address the root causes of the conflict. Radicalization occurs when individuals become disillusioned with the prospect of a peaceful resolution and resort to violence as a means of expressing their frustration, seeking justice, or pursuing their political goals. The lack of trust between Israelis and Palestinians further exacerbates the cycle of violence, as each side perceives the other as a threat.

Efforts to quell violence and foster peace have been undertaken by various actors and initiatives. Ceasefire agreements, mediated negotiations, and grassroots peacebuilding projects seek to de-escalate tensions, promote dialogue, and address the underlying causes of violence. However, sustained progress is contingent on addressing the grievances and aspirations of both Israelis and Palestinians while building trust and confidence among the parties.

2. Settlements and Land Disputes:
Settlement construction and expansion in the occupied territories remain a significant obstacle to peace. Israeli settlements in the West Bank and East Jerusalem are considered illegal under international law and have been widely condemned. The expansion of settlements not only encroaches upon Palestinian land but also undermines the prospects of a viable Palestinian state alongside Israel.

Settlements lead to disputes over land ownership, demolition of Palestinian homes, and restricted access to resources such as water and agricultural land. They also contribute to the fragmentation of the West Bank, making it increasingly challenging to establish contiguous Palestinian territories. The growth of settlements poses a significant impediment to the achievement of a two-state solution, as it erodes the territorial integrity necessary for the establishment of a sovereign and viable Palestinian state.

Efforts have been made at various levels to address the settlement issue. The international community, including the United Nations and European Union, has consistently called for a halt to settlement expansion and the dismantlement of existing settlements. These calls have been echoed by numerous resolutions and statements reaffirming the illegality of settlements. However, despite international disapproval, settlement growth continues, further complicating the prospects for a just and lasting resolution.

3. Security Concerns:

Security concerns are paramount for both Israelis and Palestinians and deeply shape the current state of affairs. Israelis rightly prioritize safeguarding their citizens from acts of terrorism and ensuring their safety. The constant threat of violence, including suicide bombings, knife attacks, and rocket strikes, has left a lasting impact on Israeli society, fostering a need for stringent security measures.

Israel's security measures include the construction of physical barriers, such as the separation barrier, and the establishment of checkpoints to control the movement of people and goods. Israel argues that these measures are necessary to prevent attacks and protect its citizens. However, Palestinians perceive these measures as an oppressive form of control and a violation of their rights. The restrictions on movement, seizures of land, and demolitions of homes have deepened resentment and contributed to the frustration of Palestinians living under occupation.

On the other hand, Palestinians endure a reality of daily restrictions, checkpoints, and limited freedom of movement due to security concerns. These measures, while intended to prevent violence, often result in a humanitarian crisis, exacerbate economic hardship, and impede access to education, healthcare, and employment opportunities. Palestinians living under occupation face systemic challenges in terms of their personal security, human rights, and
prospects for a better future.

Balancing legitimate security concerns with respect for human rights and international law is crucial to creating an environment conducive to peace and stability. Confidence-building measures, such as the gradual lifting of restrictions and better coordination between Israeli and Palestinian security forces, can help alleviate tensions and build trust.

4. Humanitarian Crisis:

The Israeli-Palestinian conflict has given rise to a significant humanitarian crisis, particularly in the Gaza Strip. The blockade imposed on Gaza has severely impacted the population, resulting in high unemployment rates, limited access to essential services, and a dire socio economic situation. The blockade restricts the entry of goods and hinders the reconstruction of vital infrastructure, exacerbating the suffering of the people living in Gaza.

The humanitarian crisis in Gaza is further compounded by the constant threat of conflict, frequent military incursions, and the insufficient delivery of aid. The lack of access to clean water, electricity, healthcare, and adequate housing heightens the vulnerability and precariousness of the lives of Gazans. According to the United Nations, Gaza could become uninhabitable by 2020 if the current situation continues.

Efforts by international humanitarian organizations, international donors, and civil society groups aim to alleviate the suffering of the Gazan population. Humanitarian aid, reconstruction projects, and initiatives to improve living conditions are ongoing. However, the deep-rooted political and security challenges underlying the crisis must be addressed for any long-term improvement to be possible.

5. Efforts towards Resolution:

Efforts to resolve the Israeli-Palestinian conflict have been pursued through various international, regional, and grassroots channels. Diplomatic initiatives, peace negotiations, and peace plans put forward by the international community, including the United Nations and countries such as the United States, have aimed to bridge the gaps between the parties.

Efforts at the international level have focused on promoting a two-state solution based on the pre-1967 borders, with mutually agreed-upon land swaps, ensuring the establishment of a viable and sovereign Palestinian state alongside Israel. However, these initiatives have faced significant challenges, including disagreement on issues such as the status of Jerusalem, the fate of Palestinian refugees, and the borders of the future states.

Civil society organizations, non-governmental organizations, and individuals committed to peace have played a significant role in fostering dialogue and understanding between Israelis and Palestinians. Grassroots movements, joint ventures, and people-to-people interactions have sought to build trust, promote empathy, and encourage cooperation at the community level. These initiatives, while often small in scale, have the potential to create a foundation for broader peacebuilding efforts.

However, despite these well-intentioned efforts, the current state of affairs remains challenging and complex. Genuine progress towards peace requires the collective commitment of all stakeholders, including the political will of Israeli and Palestinian leaders, addressing the root causes of the conflict, and finding fair and equitable solutions to the issues of violence, settlements, and security.

Conclusion:
The current state of affairs in the Israeli-Palestinian conflict underscores the urgency of finding a just and sustainable resolution. Escalating violence, settlement expansion, security concerns, and the humanitarian crisis in Gaza all contribute to the complexity and severity of the challenges facing the region. The need for dialogue, compromise, and the development of practical solutions that recognize the equality and rights of both Israelis and Palestinians is paramount.

Efforts to address the current state of affairs in the conflict require a comprehensive approach that tackles the root causes of violence, settlement expansion, and security concerns. It is essential to address the legitimate grievances and aspirations of both Israelis and Palestinians, ensuring that their rights, security, and prosperity are safeguarded.

International actors play a crucial role in supporting these efforts and promoting dialogue between the parties. The United Nations, European Union, and other regional and global organizations can provide a platform for negotiations and facilitate the implementation of agreed-upon solutions. They can also provide humanitarian assistance and support development projects that alleviate the suffering of the affected populations.

At the same time, the responsibility lies with the Israeli and Palestinian leadership to demonstrate the political will necessary for progress. Engaging in negotiations, reaching compromises, and committing to the principles of international law and human rights are essential steps towards a just and lasting peace.

Additionally, civil society organizations and grassroots peacebuilding initiatives must continue their vital work at the community level. By fostering dialogue, promoting understanding, and building trust between Israelis and Palestinians, these initiatives contribute to a broader climate of peace and coexistence.

In conclusion, the current state of affairs in the Israeli-Palestinian conflict is characterized by violence, settlement expansion, security concerns, and a humanitarian crisis. Addressing these challenges requires a comprehensive approach that addresses the root causes of the conflict, ensures the security and rights of both parties, and provides the framework for a just and lasting resolution. The collective efforts of the international community, political leaders, and civil society organizations are crucial in fostering dialogue, promoting understanding, and building the foundations for a peaceful coexistence between Israelis and Palestinians.

Living Together: Why Israel And Palestine
Must Find A Way Forward

———

Understanding the Narratives:

Israeli and Palestinian Perspectives

Introduction:

To truly grasp the intricacies of the Israeli-Palestinian conflict, a profound exploration of the narratives and perspectives upheld by Israelis and Palestinians is crucial. Understanding the historical, cultural, and political contexts that shape these narratives is key to fostering empathy, dialogue, and ultimately, finding a path towards peace. This extended chapter aims to delve even deeper into these narratives, showcasing the diverse viewpoints and shared aspirations for a better future.

Israeli Perspective:

From an Israeli perspective, the roots of the conflict extend back to the Zionist movement of the late nineteenth century, which sought to establish a homeland for the Jewish people. The Zionist movement emerged as a response to centuries of persecution, marginalization,
and discrimination faced by Jews across Europe and other parts of the world. The devastating impact of the Holocaust further intensified the desire for a secure and sovereign Jewish state. Thus, the establishment of the State of Israel in 1948 was seen as the culmination of a centuries-long struggle to find a safe haven and sanctuary for Jews.

For Israelis, the State of Israel represents a democratic, pluralistic, and vibrant society that has thrived against numerous external challenges. They view themselves as the rightful owners of the land, tying their identity as Jewish people to historical, cultural, and religious connections to the region. Jerusalem, in particular, holds profound significance for Israelis, as it is home to sites of crucial religious importance, including the Western Wall, the Church of the Holy Sepulchre, and the Al-Aqsa Mosque. Israelis argue that their claim to sovereignty over Jerusalem is not only rooted in historical and biblical narratives but also in practical terms, as they have developed and maintained the city.

The Israeli settlement enterprise in the West Bank is another point of contention. Israelis argue that these settlements are legitimate and necessary, aiming to secure strategically significant areas, protect Jewish historical sites, and ensure the country's security. They believe that the West Bank, often referred to as Judea and Samaria, is part of their biblical and ancestral homeland. However, the establishment and expansion of these settlements have been met with international criticism, as they are viewed by many as an impediment to peace and a violation of international law.

Palestinian Perspective:

From a Palestinian perspective, the Israeli-Palestinian conflict originates from the displacement and dispossession experienced by the Palestinian people following the establishment of the State of Israel. The 1948 war, known to Palestinians as the Nakba (Catastrophe), resulted in the loss of their land, homes, and livelihoods. This event led to a prolonged refugee crisis that continues to affect millions of Palestinians to this day. Palestinians argue that their right to self-determination is inherently linked to reclaiming their homeland and establishing an independent Palestinian state on the pre-1967 borders, with East Jerusalem as its capital.

The Palestinian narrative encompasses a deep sense of injustice, collective memory, and historical connection to the land. Palestinians view their struggle as one against occupation and colonization, with the Israeli presence and control over the West Bank, including East Jerusalem, as a continuous violation of their rights. The construction of Israeli settlements, the separation barrier, and military checkpoints are seen as tools of oppression, limiting Palestinians' freedom of movement, impeding economic development, and creating an environment rife with resentment, frustration, and hopelessness.

Moreover, Palestinians argue that the ongoing conflict and peace negotiations have often been asymmetrical, with significant disparities in power and influence. They assert that these inequities undermine their ability to negotiate on an equal footing and restrict their ability to shape the outcome of the conflict. Palestinians also contend that their cultural heritage and national identity have been eroded by the occupation, affecting various aspects of their lives, including access to natural resources, education, healthcare, and economic opportunities.

Shared Aspirations:

Despite the contrasting perspectives, there are shared aspirations for the future held by both Israelis and Palestinians. Both communities yearn for security, peace, and a better life for their children. They seek recognition, dignity, and freedom from violence and oppression.

Building a shared narrative necessitates recognizing and acknowledging the suffering,
narratives, and aspirations of the other side. It entails a commitment to genuine and meaningful dialogue, fostering mutual understanding, and cultivating empathy and respect. By embracing the historical and cultural narratives of each other, it becomes possible to lay the foundation for true reconciliation and a just and lasting peace.

However, reaching a shared understanding is complicated by the intricacies of the conflict and the deeply embedded narratives that have been shaped by decades of violence, trauma, and political maneuvering. The complexities stem not only from divergent interpretations of historical events but also from the different lenses through which Israelis and Palestinians view their national identities, struggles, and aspirations.

Israeli society grapples with ongoing security concerns, manifested in acts of terrorism, rocket attacks, and the threat of armed conflict. The traumatic memories of wars, suicide bombings, and constant tension influence their narrative of self-preservation and the necessity to defend their right to exist. The Israeli government argues that their actions are rooted in ensuring their citizens' security and preserving the integrity of the state amidst regional instability.

On the other hand, Palestinians face daily challenges under occupation, including restricted movement, limited access to resources, and human rights violations. Many believe that a peaceful resolution would bring about an end to their suffering, allowing them to cultivate a vibrant and thriving society. The Palestinian leadership insists that reaching a just peace agreement would provide the conditions necessary for their independence, self determination, and the fulfillment of their national aspirations.

Beyond the core issues of borders, settlements, Jerusalem, and the right of return, there are also narratives of victimhood, resilience, and the longing for justice on both sides. Israelis often recall the devastating historical persecution of Jews and the constant threats faced by Israelis as they evolved from a marginalized community to a nation-state. Palestinians, on the other hand, refer to generations of displacement, discrimination, and dispossession during the wave of Zionism and the establishment of Israel. These narratives shape their collective memory and impact their perception of the conflict.

Conclusion:

Unraveling the narratives of Israelis and Palestinians is vital to bridging the divisions and finding common ground in the pursuit of peace. Although their perspectives diverge on numerous key issues, shared aspirations for security, peace, and a better future unite both communities. By fostering dialogue, empathy, and understanding, it is possible to navigate the complex web of narratives within the Israeli-Palestinian conflict and pave the way for a
future where Israelis and Palestinians coexist in peace, security, and mutual recognition. Only through recognizing, understanding, and respecting the narratives of both sides can the seeds of reconciliation be sown, propelling all involved towards a brighter and more harmonious future.

Living Together: Why Israel And Palestine
Must Find A Way Forward

———

Challenges to Peace:

Extremism, Radicalization, and Incitement

Introduction:

In the quest for a peaceful resolution to the Israeli-Palestinian conflict, numerous challenges continue to hinder progress and perpetuate tensions. Among these challenges are extremism, radicalization, and incitement that arise from both sides of the conflict. To successfully navigate these obstacles and pave the way for peace, it is crucial to understand their roots, dynamics, and potential solutions. This chapter delves into the complexities surrounding these challenges and offers insights on how to address them in a constructive manner.

The Rise of Extremism and Radicalization:

Extremism and radicalization have become significant obstacles in the Israeli-Palestinian conflict, with deep historical and societal roots. Within both Israeli and Palestinian societies, extremist elements have emerged, often driven by a sense of injustice, frustration, and perceived existential threats. These ideologies reject compromise, fuel animosity, and promote violence as a means to achieve political objectives. The consequences of extremism are not only detrimental to the conflict resolution efforts but also pose significant security risks for all involved.

In Israeli society, right-wing extremism has gained prominence, primarily driven by nationalist ideologies and religious zealots who advocate for the expansion of Israeli settlements, reject a two-state solution, and seek to maintain Israeli control over the entire land of historic Palestine. These extremists often resort to acts of violence against Palestinians, exacerbating tensions and undermining public trust in peace processes.

On the Palestinian side, extremist factions such as Hamas and Islamic Jihad have gained popularity, particularly due to the perceived failure of diplomatic efforts and the continued Israeli occupation of Palestinian territories. These groups embrace radical Islamist ideologies, aiming to establish an Islamic state and resist Israeli occupation through armed
struggle. Their tactics, including suicide bombings and rocket attacks, contribute to a cycle of violence and hinder progress toward peaceful solutions.

Factors Driving Extremism and Radicalization:

Understanding the factors that drive extremism and radicalization is crucial in developing effective strategies to combat them. Socioeconomic grievances, political marginalization, and a lack of hope for a better future often serve as breeding grounds for extremism. In contexts where individuals face limited access to education, employment, and basic services, extremist ideologies can offer a sense of purpose and belonging.

Additionally, the historical narrative, perceived injustices, and traumas experienced by both Israelis and Palestinians play an instrumental role in radicalizing individuals. The Israeli occupation, settlement expansion, and restrictions imposed on Palestinians ignite frustration and anger, which extremist groups exploit to recruit new members. Likewise, among some Israelis, traumatic experiences such as terror attacks and the memory of the Holocaust can instill a sense of vulnerability and a desire for security, making them susceptible to extremist ideologies.

Incitement: A Barrier to Mutual Understanding:

Incitement plays a critical role in perpetuating hostility and deepening the divide between Israelis and Palestinians. It encompasses various forms, including hate speech, provocative rhetoric, and distorted narratives. Incitement thrives within educational systems, media outlets, and political platforms, indoctrinating individuals from a young age and inhibiting the development of mutual trust and empathy.

In Israeli educational institutions, there have been instances of textbooks containing biased or inflammatory content that dehumanizes Palestinians. Similarly, Palestinian textbooks have been criticized for promoting anti-Israeli sentiments and omitting historical facts that could contribute to a more nuanced understanding of the conflict. These textbooks often shape the worldview of young generations, fueling animosity and perpetuating stereotypes.

Media outlets, on both sides, have also been part of the problem, often amplifying narratives that reinforce existing biases and fuel hatred. Palestinian media has been accused of glorifying violence and promoting martyrdom, and Israeli media has been criticized for dehumanizing Palestinians and minimizing their suffering. The use of social media platforms has exacerbated this issue, allowing for the rapid spread of misinformation, propaganda, and incitement to violence among the general population.
Addressing incitement is, therefore, of utmost importance to foster an environment conducive to peace. It requires concerted efforts from both Israeli and Palestinian authorities, as well as the international community, to dismantle the systems that perpetuate incitement and promote a culture of mutual respect and understanding.

Countering Extremism and Radicalization:

To counter extremism and radicalization effectively, a comprehensive and multi dimensional approach is necessary, encompassing both short-term and long-term strategies. Firstly, addressing the systemic factors that fuel extremism, such as poverty, lack of opportunities, and political grievances, is vital. Socio Economic development initiatives focused on job creation, infrastructure improvement, and poverty alleviation can help address the underlying causes of radicalization and reduce the prospects for extremist movements to thrive.

Furthermore, engaging with moderate voices within Israeli and Palestinian societies is crucial. Empowering these individuals and groups through dialogue, education, and community initiatives can provide an alternative narrative to the extremist ideologies. By investing in peace education programs, supporting grassroots peace-building efforts, and encouraging interfaith dialogue initiatives, society can marginalize extremist elements and create a more conducive environment for peace.

Security measures are also vital to suppress extremist violence and protect civilian populations. Robust intelligence, targeted counter-terrorism operations, and border controls should be implemented cooperatively between Israeli and Palestinian security forces to prevent the infiltration of extremist elements and weapons. Simultaneously, efforts must be made to ensure that security measures do not disproportionately impact innocent civilians or further exacerbate grievances that fuel radicalization.

Overcoming Incitement:

Addressing incitement requires a multi-faceted approach involving various stakeholders and institutions. Educational reforms are essential, focusing on promoting mutual understanding, respect for diversity, and critical thinking. By revising curricula, developing educational materials that foster empathy and tolerance, and employing skilled teachers committed to promoting peace, societies can cultivate a generation that is receptive to peaceful coexistence.

Media organizations and online platforms must take responsibility for monitoring and limiting the dissemination of hate speech and false narratives. Social media companies should develop stricter content moderation policies and algorithms that detect and remove incitement-related material promptly. Collaborating with international organizations and civil society groups to enhance media literacy programs can empower individuals to identify and challenge incitement in media.

Importantly, political leaders must lead by example, encouraging dialogue, refraining from inflammatory rhetoric, and actively promoting reconciliation. Encouraging initiatives where Israeli and Palestinian communities engage in cultural exchanges, joint projects, and cooperative ventures can foster understanding, break down stereotypes, and counter the narratives that contribute to incitement.

International Cooperation and Support:

The challenges posed by extremism, radicalization, and incitement necessitate international cooperation and support. The international community, including countries, organizations, and institutions, must provide political, financial, and educational resources to combat these challenges. By sharing best practices, facilitating dialogue, and supporting programs that promote tolerance and coexistence, the global community can contribute to the establishment of a peaceful and secure future for Israelis and Palestinians.

Moreover, international involvement in conflict resolution efforts is essential to address the underlying issues contributing to extremism and radicalization. By actively engaging with

Israeli and Palestinian leaders, assisting in mediation processes, and upholding international law, the international community can play a crucial role in fostering an environment conducive to lasting peace.

Conclusion:

Challenges to peace in the Israeli-Palestinian conflict, such as extremism, radicalization, and incitement, are deeply entrenched and complex issues. However, addressing these challenges is imperative for achieving a lasting resolution. By Implementing comprehensive approaches that target the root causes of extremism, promoting dialogue and understanding, and countering incitement, progress can be made towards a more peaceful future.

It is important to acknowledge that addressing extremism, radicalization, and incitement is not a one-sided endeavor. Both Israeli and Palestinian societies must work collaboratively to combat these challenges and promote a culture of peace. This requires a willingness to engage in dialogue, mutual respect, and a shared commitment to finding common ground.
To effectively counter extremism and radicalization, it is crucial to invest in education and socio-economic development initiatives that create opportunities for individuals and reduce the appeal of extremist ideologies. By improving access to quality education, providing job opportunities, and addressing political grievances, societies can offer viable alternatives to extremist narratives and prevent radicalization.

Engaging with moderate voices within Israeli and Palestinian societies is also instrumental in countering extremism. By empowering these individuals and promoting their ideas, society can marginalize extremist elements and create a more inclusive and tolerant environment. Initiatives such as peace education programs, interfaith dialogue, and grassroots peacebuilding efforts can foster understanding, empathy, and cooperation among different communities.

In parallel with these efforts, security measures must be implemented to suppress extremist violence and protect civilians. Effective intelligence gathering, targeted counter-terrorism operations, and border controls are necessary to prevent the infiltration of extremist elements and the proliferation of weapons. However, it is essential to ensure that these measures are implemented in a way that upholds human rights, avoids disproportionate impacts on innocent civilians, and does not exacerbate grievances.

Addressing incitement requires a multi-stakeholder approach involving educational institutions, media organizations, online platforms, and political leaders. Educational reforms focused on promoting mutual understanding, critical thinking, and respect for diversity are crucial in cultivating a generation that rejects extremism. Media organizations and social media companies must take responsibility for monitoring and limiting the dissemination of hate speech and false narratives.

Political leaders must lead by example and actively promote reconciliation, refraining from inflammatory rhetoric and encouraging dialogue. Encouraging initiatives that promote cultural exchanges and cooperation between Israeli and Palestinian communities can help break down stereotypes and counter the narratives that contribute to incitement.

International cooperation and support play a significant role in addressing the challenges of extremism, radicalization, and incitement. The international community should provide political, financial, and educational resources to combat these issues and support the establishment of a peaceful future for Israelis and Palestinians. Sharing best practices, facilitating dialogue, and upholding international law are crucial in promoting understanding and fostering an environment conducive to peace.

While the challenges of extremism, radicalization, and incitement may seem daunting, it is essential to remain committed to the pursuit of peace. By understanding the roots and dynamics of these challenges and implementing multi-dimensional strategies, progress can be made towards a peaceful resolution to the Israeli-Palestinian conflict. It requires the collective effort of Israeli and Palestinian societies, as well as the support and involvement of the international community, to overcome these obstacles and build a future of peace and coexistence.

Living Together: Why Israel And Palestine
Must Find A Way Forward

———

The Way Forward:

Practical Solutions for Coexistence and Peaceful Cohabitation

Introduction:

In the face of a protracted and deeply entrenched conflict, it is imperative to delve into practical solutions for coexistence and peaceful cohabitation between the Israeli and Palestinian peoples. The path to achieving lasting peace may seem daunting, but it remains necessary for the well-being and prosperity of both societies. This chapter will explore practical approaches that can pave the way forward, fostering an environment of mutual understanding, tolerance, and respect.

Building Trust:

Building trust is essential for lasting peace. It requires concerted efforts at various levels, from grassroots initiatives to high-level negotiations. Encouraging face-to-face interaction and dialogue through programs like person-to-person encounters, cultural exchanges, and joint projects can help humanize the "other" and create opportunities for shared experiences. These initiatives break down walls of prejudice and stereotypes, foster empathy, and build trust. Additionally, confidence-building measures, such as the release of prisoners as a goodwill gesture, can help build trust among the parties involved.

Addressing Core Issues:

To achieve sustainable peace, it is vital to address the core issues at the heart of the Israeli Palestinian conflict. These include the question of borders, the status of Jerusalem, the right of return for Palestinian refugees, and the issue of settlements. Creative and inclusive solutions, considering the aspirations and fears of all parties involved, must be explored.

An equitable agreement on borders should be the foundation of any future peace deal and should reflect the demographic realities on the ground. It should ensure territorial integrity and security for both Israelis and Palestinians, while also taking into account the needs of settlements located near the border areas. Dialogue and negotiation are key to finding a
balance that respects the rights and aspirations of both sides.

Sharing Jerusalem as a capital for both states is a significant challenge that requires sensitivity and creativity. Jerusalem holds immense religious and cultural significance for Jews, Christians, and Muslims alike. It is crucial to find arrangements that respect and accommodate the religious and cultural aspirations of all parties involved. This may involve a special status for Jerusalem under international oversight, allowing free access to religious sites while ensuring that both Israeli and Palestinian claims are respected.

Addressing the right of return for Palestinian refugees is a highly sensitive and complex issue. Recognizing their legitimate aspirations while also taking into account the security concerns of Israelis is essential. Constructive discussions should explore practical solutions that respect Palestinian aspirations, such as compensation, acknowledgment of historical injustices, and the possibility of family reunification within the borders of a Palestinian state. It is crucial to find a balance that ensures the security and demographic integrity of Israel while acknowledging the rights and dignity of Palestinian refugees.

The issue of settlements presents significant challenges. A practical solution would require a phased and coordinated approach for dismantling illegal settlements, reducing the potential for disturbances and violence. This process should be accompanied by sufficient compensation and support for Israeli settlers who are willing to relocate, while ensuring that the rights and aspirations of Palestinians in the occupied territories are protected. International assistance and oversight can help facilitate this process.

Security Cooperation:

Ensuring the security of Israelis and Palestinians is paramount in any peace process. Establishing a cooperative and coordinated security framework is imperative. Both sides must work together to combat terrorism, maintain law and order, and prevent violent incidents from undermining trust-building efforts. This cooperation includes sharing intelligence, coordinating joint patrols, and even developing joint training programs to enhance the capabilities of Palestinian security forces. Confidence-building measures should include reciprocal initiatives to demonstrate commitment to peace and stability, such as the joint training of Israeli and Palestinian security forces.

Furthermore, phased and mutually agreed-upon withdrawals of Israeli forces from the occupied territories, coordinated with the strengthening of Palestinian security institutions, can help assuage fears and build confidence in the prospect of lasting security. International support for capacity-building efforts and the provision of resources for the development of Palestinian security infrastructure are vital.
Economic Development:

Economic development is crucial for stability and peace. Promoting economic cooperation and investment between Israeli and Palestinian businesses can create opportunities for growth and prosperity. Joint industrial zones, trade agreements, and increased access to markets can help alleviate poverty, reduce unemployment, and promote interdependence, binding the two societies together in shared economic interests. Economic cooperation also provides opportunities for individuals from both sides to engage in economic activities together, fostering social integration and mutual understanding.

International donors, regional partners, and economic experts must collaborate to design and implement strategies that support economic development, infrastructure projects, and job creation. Supporting entrepreneurship, small and medium enterprises, and cross-border economic ventures can foster economic interdependence, which is crucial for the sustainability of peaceful coexistence. Initiatives should prioritize investment in sectors such as renewable energy, agriculture, technology, and tourism, which have the potential to create sustainable economic growth and prosperity for both Israelis and Palestinians.

Education for Peace:

Promoting peace education from an early age is crucial to fostering a culture of coexistence and tolerance. Educational institutions on both sides play a vital role in shaping the attitudes and perceptions of future generations. It is essential to revise school curricula, eliminating biased narratives and stereotypes, and embracing a balanced and inclusive approach that promotes empathy and understanding.

Promoting historical accuracy, highlighting shared history, positive aspects of each other's cultures, and emphasizing the importance of mutual respect and understanding can counteract the cycle of animosity. Educational programs should encourage critical thinking, empathy, and open-mindedness, enabling young people to challenge stereotypes and prejudices. Engaging teachers in professional development programs, international exchanges, and joint educational projects can enhance their ability to deliver inclusive and peace-oriented education. Moreover, encouraging joint educational initiatives, where Israeli and Palestinian students come together in classrooms or engage in cultural exchange programs, can help dispel misconceptions and forge lifelong friendships, laying the foundation for a harmonious future.

International Support and Mediation:
The international community has a significant role to play in facilitating a just and lasting peace. Sustained support for peacebuilding initiatives, both financially and through technical assistance, is vital. International actors should collaborate with local and regional stakeholders to enhance community-driven projects that promote dialogue, trust-building, and sustainable development.

Furthermore, international mediation efforts, led by impartial actors, can help bridge gaps between Israelis and Palestinians. Mediators should work closely with both Israeli and Palestinian leaderships, utilizing their influence to encourage compromise and the implementation of practical solutions. Engaging regional powers and other relevant actors can bolster the credibility of the peace process and contribute to a comprehensive and inclusive resolution.

Conclusion:

Achieving coexistence and peaceful cohabitation between Israelis and Palestinians is a complex endeavor, requiring thoughtful consideration, dedication, and resilience. Through building trust, addressing core issues, fostering security cooperation, promoting economic development, educating for peace, and receiving international support, a path toward a peaceful resolution can be forged.

It is essential to acknowledge the historical complexities and grievances of both sides while focusing on shared values and future opportunities. The way forward may be challenging, but the potential benefits of coexistence – social, economic, and cultural – are immense. It is time for all stakeholders to embrace practical solutions that promote understanding, respect, and a shared vision of peace for future generations.

Living Together: Why Israel And Palestine
Must Find A Way Forward

———

Economic Cooperation:

Opportunities for Growth and Stability

Introduction:

In the Israeli-Palestinian conflict, economic cooperation has often been overshadowed by the prevailing political tensions. However, looking beyond the conflicts, it is crucial to recognize the immense potential for economic collaboration between Israelis and Palestinians. Economic cooperation has the power to foster growth, stability, and ultimately contribute to the building of a peaceful coexistence between these two intertwined societies. This chapter explores the opportunities that arise when economic interests are prioritized and when both sides recognize the significant benefits of working together.

Investment Opportunities:

One of the most promising aspects of economic cooperation in the Israeli-Palestinian context is the possibility of attracting foreign investments. The region possesses a highly educated workforce, advanced technology sectors, and a strategic geographic location. By leveraging these advantages, both Israelis and Palestinians can attract foreign capital and expertise to drive economic growth.

Foreign investments can be utilized to develop infrastructure projects, including the construction of transportation networks, energy facilities, and telecommunication systems. These investments would not only create much-needed job opportunities for Palestinians but also ensure that the region has the necessary resources to support economic growth. For instance, investment in renewable energy projects such as solar farms and wind turbines can address the energy needs of both Israelis and Palestinians while also contributing to global efforts to combat climate change.

Furthermore, investments in high-tech industries and innovation hubs can stimulate entrepreneurship and the development of cutting-edge technologies. This collaboration in the field of innovation can lead to the creation of new startups and give rise to mutually beneficial partnerships, promoting economic growth and technological advancements for both societies. By creating an environment that attracts investment, the Israeli-Palestinian region can unlock its economic potential and position itself as a key player in the global economy.

Trade and Market Access:

Economic cooperation can also enable increased trade between Israel and Palestine. By establishing trade agreements and facilitating the movement of goods and services, the two parties can mutually benefit from expanded market access. Enhanced trade relations not only encourage economic growth but also foster interdependence and create shared interests, which can serve as incentives for maintaining stability and peace in the long run.

To facilitate trade, it is crucial to improve the efficiency of customs procedures, streamline regulations, and invest in border infrastructure. By reducing bureaucratic barriers and facilitating the movement of goods and people, trade can flourish, benefiting both Israelis and Palestinians. Furthermore, expanding trade beyond the immediate region can open up new market opportunities for local businesses, fostering economic diversification and resilience.

Encouraging the participation of small and medium enterprises (SMEs) in trade can play a significant role in promoting economic cooperation. Governments and international organizations should collaborate to provide capacity-building programs, access to finance, and technical assistance to empower SMEs to engage in cross-border trade. This support would enable smaller businesses to benefit from trade opportunities and contribute to sustainable economic development.

Business Partnerships and Joint Ventures:

Joining forces through business partnerships and joint ventures offers countless possibilities for Israelis and Palestinians to collaborate. By pooling resources, knowledge, and expertise, they can access new markets, develop innovative products, and strengthen their competitive advantage on the global stage. Joint ventures can also help bridge cultural and societal gaps, promoting a deeper understanding and appreciation of each other's perspectives and contributing to a healthier relationship between the two communities.

Collaboration in research and development can be particularly valuable in promoting business partnerships. By investing in joint research programs and innovation centers, Israelis and Palestinians can leverage their complementary strengths in areas such as biotechnology, medicine, agriculture, and environmental sustainability. These partnerships
can lead to breakthrough discoveries, contribute to economic growth, and foster a spirit of cooperation and shared goals.

Cross-Border Infrastructure:

The creation of cross-border infrastructure projects is another avenue through which economic cooperation can thrive. Establishing shared transportation networks, energy grids, and water management systems can generate economic benefits for both Israelis and Palestinians. These ventures can improve access to essential services, stimulate trade, and facilitate the movement of goods, thereby creating an environment conducive to stability and prosperity.

Cross-border transportation projects, such as the construction of highways, railway lines, and bridges, can enhance connectivity between different regions and streamline travel and trade routes. Additionally, shared energy grids can optimize resource allocation and promote the efficient distribution of electricity. By jointly managing water resources through infrastructure projects, both sides can reduce reliance on scarce water supplies and work towards sustainable water management, benefiting agriculture, industry, and communities on both sides.

Supporting Small and Medium Enterprises:
The development and support of small and medium enterprises (SMEs) emerge as a vital component in promoting economic cooperation. Encouraging entrepreneurship and providing training, mentoring, and financial support for startups not only empower individuals but also contribute to the overall economic growth and stability. Supporting SMEs can lead to job creation, boost local economies, and empower marginalized communities, thereby reducing inequalities and improving social cohesion.

One effective way to support SMEs is through the establishment of business incubators and entrepreneurial centers, providing access to mentoring, training, and networking opportunities. These platforms can facilitate the exchange of ideas, foster collaboration, and create an ecosystem that supports the growth and success of startups in both Israeli and Palestinian communities. Additionally, access to microfinance and tailored financial products can enable SMEs to access capital and overcome challenges associated with limited resources.

Regional Economic Integration:
While focusing on bilateral economic cooperation is essential, it is crucial to consider the wider regional context. Engaging neighboring countries in joint economic ventures and collaborative initiatives can create a more connected and

prosperous regional economy. By fostering regional economic integration, Israelis and Palestinians can tap into the collective potential for growth, stability, and increased cooperation. Regional economic integration can help break down barriers, build trust, and lay the groundwork for long lasting peace and stability.

Regional economic integration initiatives can include the establishment of free trade zones, harmonization of regulations, and mutual recognition of standards, facilitating the movement of goods and services across borders. By collaborating in areas such as infrastructure development, tourism promotion, and renewable energy projects, neighboring countries can create interdependencies that provide incentives for peaceful coexistence and cooperation.

Organizations such as the World Bank, the United Nations, and regional economic bodies should play an active role in facilitating regional economic integration initiatives. Through financial and technical support, they can help create an enabling environment for economic cooperation, providing expertise, investment, and knowledge-sharing platforms. Additionally, the involvement of regional governments and stakeholders through dialogue platforms and joint decision-making can strengthen regional economic integration efforts.

Education and Skills Development:
To fully leverage economic cooperation opportunities, investments in education and skills development play a pivotal role. By equipping the workforce with relevant skills and knowledge, both Israelis and Palestinians can increase their competitiveness, adapt to rapidly evolving industries, and foster innovation.

Education systems in the region should prioritize technical and vocational training programs that align with market needs. These programs should focus on providing practical skills that can enhance employability and entrepreneurship. Collaboration between Israeli and Palestinian educational institutions can facilitate knowledge exchange and the development of joint curricula that address shared economic challenges and opportunities.

Furthermore, investing in vocational training and entrepreneurship education for marginalized communities, including women and youth, can foster inclusivity and socioeconomic empowerment. By breaking down gender barriers, enhancing access to education, and promoting inclusive hiring practices, economic cooperation can contribute to the advancement of gender equality and social cohesion.

Conclusion:

Economic cooperation offers significant opportunities for growth and stability in the Israeli Palestinian context. By looking beyond the political disputes and prioritizing economic interests, Israelis and Palestinians can unlock their shared potential and build a foundation for peaceful coexistence. The opportunities for cooperation are vast, ranging from attracting foreign investments to expanding trade, fostering business partnerships and joint ventures, developing cross-border infrastructure, supporting SMEs, promoting regional economic integration, and investing in education and skills development.

However, it is important to acknowledge that economic cooperation alone cannot solve the complex issues underlying the Israeli-Palestinian conflict. Political, social, and cultural factors also need to be addressed to achieve lasting peace and stability. Nevertheless, economic cooperation can act as a catalyst for positive change, creating a conducive environment for dialogue, trust-building, and the gradual resolution of political disputes.

To effectively promote economic cooperation, it is vital for both Israeli and Palestinian authorities to demonstrate a genuine commitment to collaboration. This requires the establishment of clear policies, regulatory frameworks, and incentives that foster economic integration, as well as the removal of barriers and obstacles that hinder cross-border economic activities.

Furthermore, international actors, such as the United Nations, the European Union, and regional economic organizations, should play a supportive role in facilitating economic cooperation initiatives. They can provide financial assistance, technical expertise, and diplomatic support, helping to bridge divides and create opportunities for dialogue and collaboration.

Ultimately, economic cooperation can contribute to the shared prosperity and stability of Israelis and Palestinians. By prioritizing economic interests, investing in infrastructure, supporting entrepreneurship, and enhancing regional integration, both societies can move towards a future that is defined by mutual understanding, shared prosperity, and peaceful coexistence. It is by seizing these economic opportunities and transcending the political impasse that a brighter and more sustainable future can be realized for all.

Living Together: Why Israel And Palestine
Must Find A Way Forward

———

Cultural Exchange:

Building Bridges and Fostering Understanding

Introduction:

In the midst of the Israeli-Palestinian conflict, cultural exchange plays a significant role in fostering understanding, bridging gaps, and building a foundation for peace. People from different cultures coming together to share experiences, traditions, and values opens up avenues for dialogue, empathy, and the recognition of our shared humanity. This chapter explores the power of cultural exchange as a transformative tool to transcend barriers, break down stereotypes, and cultivate a sense of unity and coexistence.

1. The Importance of Cultural Exchange:

Cultural exchange serves as a means to dismantle prejudices and misconceptions that have long fueled the Israeli-Palestinian conflict. It offers a platform for individuals to engage in open dialogue and interact through the lens of culture, encouraging empathy, appreciation, and respect for one another's unique identities. Through the exchange of art, music, literature, cuisine, and language, cultural barriers are broken down, leading to deeper connections and understanding.

It is essential to understand that cultural exchange should not be seen as a panacea for resolving the conflict, but rather as a vital step towards building trust, empathy, and understanding among communities. This process requires active participation, willingness to learn and unlearn, and a commitment to embracing the values of diversity and coexistence.

2. Art as a Catalyst for Change:

Art has always been a powerful medium for expressing emotions, thoughts, and perspectives. It can transcend language barriers, serving as a common language that unites people from different backgrounds. In the context of the Israeli-Palestinian conflict, art offers a safe space for dialogue, allowing artists to share their stories and experiences in a way that promotes empathy and compassion.
Art exhibits, cultural festivals, and joint artistic ventures can play a pivotal role in humanizing the "other" and creating a sense of shared purpose. These shared platforms enable artists to challenge stereotypes and engage with difficult topics while fostering understanding and empathy among diverse audiences. Such art initiatives can also highlight the beauty and richness of each culture, fostering appreciation and respect.

Artistic collaborations between Israeli and Palestinian artists can be particularly powerful, as they showcase the potential for cooperation and mutual respect. It is through engaging in joint art projects, such as mural paintings, theatrical performances, or poetry readings, that artists can both celebrate their distinct cultural identities and find common ground for shared narratives of peace and coexistence.

3. Education and Cultural Exchange:

Integrating cultural exchange programs into educational institutions is instrumental in breaking down walls of ignorance and fostering understanding among the younger generation. By exposing students to diverse perspectives, narratives, and historical contexts, they can develop critical thinking skills and empathy.

It is crucial to emphasize accurate and comprehensive education that acknowledges the historical complexities and grievances of both the Israeli and Palestinian people. By providing students with a well-rounded understanding of the conflict, cultural exchange programs help foster empathy and pave the way for future generations committed to peace and coexistence.

It is equally important to encourage cross-cultural friendships, exchange programs, and joint educational initiatives within schools. These connections allow for genuine relationships to form, breaking down stereotypes and building bridges based on shared experiences and common goals. By engaging students in dialogue, collaborative projects, and guided discussions, cultural exchange programs can create spaces for genuine understanding, empathy, and collaboration.

4. Media and Cultural Exchange:

Media has the power to shape public opinion and influence perceptions. Therefore, it is crucial for media outlets to promote accurate and balanced depictions of both Israeli and Palestinian culture, acting as catalysts for fostering understanding.

Journalists, filmmakers, and content creators should strive to tell human stories that
transcend political divisions, highlighting the shared values, joys, and aspirations of individuals on both sides. By humanizing conflicting narratives, the media can contribute to building bridges and promoting a deeper understanding of the complexities of the conflict.

Moreover, media organizations should actively encourage and support joint productions and collaborations between Israeli and Palestinian artists and filmmakers. These collaborations can showcase the power of cultural exchange and serve as a testament to the shared aspirations and desires for peace among people on both sides.

The use of social media platforms should also be leveraged for facilitating cultural exchange. By creating online spaces for dialogue, collaboration, and the sharing of artistic creations, individuals from different backgrounds can engage in meaningful interactions, fostering empathy, and promoting understanding on a global scale.

5. Grassroots Initiatives and Cultural Exchange:

Grassroots initiatives are vital in facilitating cultural exchange at the community level. These initiatives can take various forms, such as joint music ensembles, intercultural cooking classes, storytelling workshops, or language exchange programs. By bringing people together in a non-political environment, these initiatives break down barriers, foster dialogue, and cultivate empathy.

Creating spaces where people can engage in authentic conversations and interactions, irrespective of their social, political, or religious identity, allows for genuine understanding to grow. By prioritizing shared values and interests, grassroots initiatives can transcend the conflicts and divisions that have plagued Israeli and Palestinian societies, opening up the possibility for collaboration and peaceful coexistence.

It is crucial to support and amplify grassroots initiatives led by local community leaders, artists, educators, and activists who are committed to promoting cultural exchange and dialogue. These initiatives often have a deep understanding of the context, challenges, and aspirations of the communities they serve, making them effective catalysts for positive change.

Conclusion:

Cultural exchange provides a unique avenue for people to come together, regardless of their backgrounds, and find common

ground. By valuing and embracing the richness of diverse cultures, we foster an environment of respect, empathy, and understanding. Through art, education, media, and grassroots initiatives, we have the opportunity to build bridges
and overcome the obstacles of the Israeli-Palestinian conflict.

It is through these small acts of connection, dialogue, and collaboration that we can collectively work towards a future of coexistence, peace, and harmony in the region. By engaging in cultural exchange, we acknowledge the humanity in one another, creating a foundation for a shared and prosperous future. Let us embrace the power of cultural exchange and remember that our differences, when celebrated and understood, can be the catalyst for building a more inclusive and peaceful society.
Living Together: Why Israel And Palestine
Must Find A Way Forward

———

Political Dialogue:

Rebuilding Trust and Exploring Compromise

Introduction:

In the Israeli-Palestinian conflict, political dialogue plays a critical role in addressing the deep-rooted grievances and reaching a sustainable solution. Open and constructive discussions are essential for rebuilding trust and exploring compromise. This chapter delves deeper into the importance of dialogue, methods to rebuild trust, avenues for genuine engagement, the significance of addressing core issues, the role of mediation and facilitation, the exploration of compromise, the involvement of civil society, the implementation of confidence-building measures, and the lessons learned from successful peace processes in other regions.

1. The Importance of Dialogue:

Political dialogue serves as a vital tool for conflict resolution, allowing conflicting parties to express their concerns, grievances, and aspirations. It provides a platform for meaningful engagement and the opportunity to build mutual understanding. By engaging in dialogue, both Israelis and Palestinians can feel heard and validated, paving the way for the resolution of their longstanding dispute.

Dialogue allows for the exploration of different perspectives and the exchange of ideas. It fosters empathy, humanizes the conflict, and helps debunk stereotypes and misunderstandings. Additionally, dialogue enables the identification of shared interests and common ground, offering the potential for mutually beneficial solutions that may have otherwise been overlooked.

2. Rebuilding Trust:

Trust is an essential component of any successful negotiation or peace process. In the context of the Israeli-Palestinian conflict, trust has been eroded over decades of violence, mistrust, and broken promises. Rebuilding trust requires sincerity, transparency, and a commitment to honoring agreements made.

To rebuild trust, it is crucial for both Israeli and Palestinian leaders to engage in genuine and meaningful dialogue. This involves setting aside preconceived notions and prejudices, actively listening to the concerns of the other side, and demonstrating a willingness to find common ground. Open and honest communication can help repair the damaged trust between the parties, laying the foundation for a sustainable peace.

Building trust also necessitates addressing the injustices of the past and acknowledging historical narratives. By recognizing the legitimate concerns and aspirations of both Israelis and Palestinians, leaders can create an environment where trust can gradually be rebuilt. This may involve the establishment of truth and reconciliation commissions, where individuals affected by the conflict can share their experiences and work towards healing and reconciliation.

3. Genuine Engagement:

In the Israeli-Palestinian conflict, genuine engagement goes beyond mere rhetoric. It requires leaders to go above and beyond their political affiliations and personal biases, putting the interests of their people and the region as a whole at the forefront. Genuine engagement involves robust and constructive discussions, where leaders engage in difficult conversations, acknowledge the pain and suffering experienced by both sides, and commit to finding mutually acceptable solutions.

Genuine engagement implies recognizing and embracing the complexity of the conflict. It requires leaders to step outside their comfort zones and engage in dialogue with a willingness to question their own assumptions and deeply held beliefs. Leaders must also prioritize inclusivity, ensuring that diverse voices are heard and respected. This includes involving women, youth, marginalized communities, and civil society organizations as key actors in the dialogue, as their perspectives and experiences are integral to understanding the multifaceted nature of the conflict.

Addressing the root causes of the conflict and its wider regional implications is another crucial aspect of genuine engagement. Leaders need to acknowledge the broader geopolitical dynamics, such as the impact of regional actors and international relationships, and explore avenues for regional cooperation and collaboration. By considering the larger context, comprehensive and sustainable solutions can be pursued.

4. Addressing Core Issues:
Political dialogue must focus on addressing the core issues at the heart of the conflict, such as borders, settlements, the status of Jerusalem, and the right of return for Palestinian refugees. These sensitive topics require thoughtful and respectful discussions to find mutually acceptable solutions.

Negotiations should involve compromise on each side, recognizing the need for self determination, security, and dignity for both Israelis and Palestinians. Creative solutions may be explored, such as establishing a demilitarized Palestinian state alongside appropriate security measures for Israel, or developing shared governance models for Jerusalem that respect the religious and cultural sensitivities of all parties involved.

It is important to recognize that addressing core issues extends beyond political negotiations. Economic, social, and cultural aspects should be part of the dialogue as well. This includes addressing socio-economic disparities, promoting economic cooperation, fostering mutual understanding through cultural exchanges, and ensuring equitable access to resources for both Israelis and Palestinians.

Furthermore, dialogue should encourage discussions about the experiences and needs of vulnerable groups, such as refugees, internally displaced persons, and minorities. Their perspectives and grievances deserve attention and consideration in shaping a comprehensive solution that is just and inclusive.

5. Mediation and Facilitation:

The involvement of impartial third-party mediators can enhance the effectiveness of political dialogue. Mediators, including international organizations or respected individuals, can provide a neutral platform for negotiations, offer expert guidance, and assist in bridging the gaps between the parties.

To ensure the effectiveness of mediation, mediators must possess a deep understanding of the history, emotions, and complexities surrounding the conflict. They should encourage dialogue between all relevant stakeholders, including political leaders, civil society organizations, religious leaders, and grassroots movements. By facilitating a comprehensive and inclusive approach to mediation, all voices can be heard, leading to more sustainable and inclusive outcomes.

Mediators should help identify areas of common interest and shared values among the conflicting parties. They must also

ensure the transparency and integrity of the negotiation process, keeping the lines of communication open and maintaining the confidentiality necessary for productive discussions. Additionally, mediators can provide technical
expertise, legal advice, and creative proposals to overcome impasses and promote forward movement.

6. Exploring Compromise:

Compromise is an integral part of any negotiation process. It requires a willingness to let go of absolute demands and search for mutually beneficial solutions. This may involve creative solutions, such as land swaps, shared sovereignty, or joint economic ventures, that address the needs and aspirations of both Israelis and Palestinians.

Compromise also requires acknowledging the need for transitional and confidence-building measures. By implementing interim agreements or phased approaches, both parties can test the feasibility of proposed solutions, build trust, and pave the way for wider and more comprehensive agreements.

During the exploratory phase of compromise, it is crucial for negotiators to consider the various perspectives and needs of the people they represent. This involves conducting inclusive consultations, engaging civil society organizations, and ensuring that the proposed compromises are in line with international law, human rights principles, and the aspirations of the broader population.

7. Including Civil Society:

In addition to political leaders, civil society groups, activists, and grassroots organizations play a crucial role in fostering dialogue and promoting peace. Their involvement ensures the inclusion of diverse perspectives and a broader representation of the people affected by the conflict.

Civil society organizations can act as conduits for citizen input, expressing the aspirations, needs, and concerns of their respective communities. They can help bridge the gap between political leaders and the people they represent, creating a sense of ownership and accountability. Engaging civil society in the dialogue process fosters a participatory democracy where decisions are influenced, guided, and supported by the voices of those directly affected by the conflict.

To foster an inclusive dialogue, civil society organizations should be empowered and supported through capacity-building initiatives, funding opportunities, and platforms for advocacy. Efforts should be made to ensure the inclusion of marginalized groups such as women, youth, refugees, and religious and ethnic minorities. By Including these diverse voices, the dialogue process becomes more comprehensive, representative, and ultimately,
effective in addressing the root causes of the conflict.

Civil society organizations can also play a critical role in building trust and promoting understanding between communities. Through grassroots initiatives, cultural exchanges, and dialogue programs, they can facilitate interactions and connections between Israelis and Palestinians at the grassroots level. These interactions humanize the "other" and create opportunities for empathy, understanding, and the recognition of shared values and aspirations.

Furthermore, civil society organizations can provide important expertise and technical knowledge in areas such as conflict resolution, transitional justice, and peacebuilding. They can help shape inclusive policies and solutions, ensuring the sustainability and implementation of agreements reached during political dialogue.

8. Confidence-Building Measures:

Confidence-building measures are vital in the Israeli-Palestinian conflict, as they contribute to the rebuilding of trust and provide tangible proof of progress and commitment to the dialogue process. These measures are aimed at creating a positive atmosphere, reducing tensions, and demonstrating a genuine intention to resolve the conflict.

Confidence-building measures can include steps such as the release of prisoners, easing restrictions on movement and access, joint economic initiatives, and enhancement of security cooperation. These measures should be implemented in a phased approach, allowing incremental progress and building upon each other.

Furthermore, confidence-building measures should address the immediate needs and concerns of the population affected by the conflict. This could involve measures to improve living conditions, address socio-economic disparities, promote freedom of movement and access to resources, and protect human rights. By addressing the daily realities and needs of the people, confidence is built in the sincerity and commitment of the parties involved.

9. Lessons from Successful Peace Processes:

While each conflict has its unique dynamics, there are valuable lessons to be learned from successful peace processes in other regions. For example, the Northern Ireland peace process, the South African transition to democracy, and the Colombia peace process all provide insights into the importance of political dialogue, compromise, and the engagement of civil society.
These successful peace processes have demonstrated the significance of inclusive dialogue, where all relevant stakeholders have a voice and representation. They show the necessity of addressing core issues, recognizing and acknowledging historical grievances, and finding creative solutions that meet the needs

and aspirations of all parties involved.

Moreover, these processes highlight the importance of transitional and confidence-building measures, as well as the critical role of mediation and facilitation in overcoming impasses and bridging divides. The lessons learned from these processes can inform and inspire the Israeli-Palestinian conflict resolution efforts.

Conclusion:

Political dialogue plays a crucial role in the Israeli-Palestinian conflict, serving as a platform for rebuilding trust and exploring compromise. Genuine engagement, addressing core issues, and including civil society are essential elements for a successful dialogue process. Mediation and facilitation can enhance the effectiveness of the process, while confidence building measures create a positive atmosphere and demonstrate commitment. By learning from the successes of other peace processes, the path to a sustainable solution in the Israeli-Palestinian conflict becomes more clear.

Living Together: Why Israel And Palestine
Must Find A Way Forward

———

The Role of the International Community in Resolving the Conflict

Introduction:

The Israeli-Palestinian conflict has long been a contentious issue that has garnered international attention. The involvement of the international community in this protracted conflict is essential, as it plays a crucial role in facilitating dialogue, supporting peace initiatives, and providing humanitarian assistance. Recognizing the significance of this conflict beyond its regional boundaries, numerous countries and international organizations have dedicated significant efforts towards its resolution. This chapter explores the extensive role of the international community in resolving the Israeli-Palestinian conflict, delving deeper into specific strategies, challenges, and potential avenues for effective engagement.

1. Diplomatic Mediation:

Diplomatic mediation is one of the primary roles of the international community in resolving the Israeli-Palestinian conflict. Neutral third-party mediators, often from international organizations or countries with no direct stake in the conflict, work towards facilitating dialogue and negotiations between Israeli and Palestinian representatives. These mediators engage in shuttle diplomacy, moving between the parties and maintaining confidentiality to encourage candid discussions and foster trust. By serving as impartial intermediaries, they help bridge the gap and facilitate a greater understanding of each side's concerns, aspirations, and red lines. With their expertise and knowledge of conflict resolution, these mediators can propose creative compromises and encourage parties to explore potential resolutions.

However, diplomatic mediation faces various challenges. The deep-rooted mistrust between the parties, historical grievances, and the high stakes involved often impede progress. Additionally, political changes, leadership transitions, and shifting geopolitical dynamics can impact the continuity and effectiveness of mediation efforts. Nevertheless, the international community's commitment and perseverance in diplomatic mediation can ultimately contribute to narrowing differences, building confidence, and fostering an
environment conducive to productive negotiations.

2. Support for Peace Initiatives:

The international community plays a pivotal role in supporting peace initiatives aimed at resolving the Israeli-Palestinian conflict. From the Camp David Accords in 1978 to the Oslo Accords in 1993, these initiatives have provided frameworks for negotiations and outlined potential solutions to the outstanding issues between the parties. International actors rally behind these initiatives, offering political, economic, and technical support to ensure their success. They provide expertise in areas such as governance, security, and legal frameworks, which are crucial for building a sustainable peace process.

Furthermore, the international community mobilizes financial resources to support peace building efforts. Donor conferences and financial aid help strengthen institutions, develop infrastructure, and address socioeconomic inequalities that fuel the conflict. These investments not only contribute to the stability and prosperity of the region but also demonstrate the international community's commitment to a just and lasting resolution.

Yet, the implementation of peace initiatives faces significant challenges. Disagreements over final status issues, security concerns, and internal divisions within both the Israeli and Palestinian leaderships often hamper progress. Moreover, the political landscape can change rapidly, rendering existing initiatives obsolete or requiring their adaptation. Nevertheless, the international community's consistent support for peace initiatives demonstrates its determination to manifest a viable and comprehensive resolution to the Israeli-Palestinian conflict.

3. Humanitarian Assistance:

One of the immediate concerns for the international community is providing humanitarian assistance to the affected populations in the Israeli-Palestinian conflict. Decades of protracted violence have resulted in numerous humanitarian crises, including displacement, food insecurity, inadequate healthcare, and infrastructural challenges. Countries and international organizations have stepped in to alleviate the suffering caused by the conflict, offering emergency relief, development aid, and assistance in rebuilding essential infrastructure. They prioritize vital sectors such as health, education, water, and sanitation, addressing immediate needs while simultaneously establishing a foundation for long-term development.

The provision of humanitarian assistance not only addresses the immediate consequences of the conflict but also serves as a gesture of goodwill. Such gestures promote empathy
and understanding between communities, facilitating a conducive environment for dialogue and reconciliation. Additionally, humanitarian aid can help build rapport and trust between the international community and the parties involved, laying the groundwork for future cooperation towards

sustainable peace.

However, delivering humanitarian aid in conflict zones is not without challenges. Access restrictions imposed by both parties, bureaucratic hurdles, and security risks often complicate the delivery of essential services to those in need. Furthermore, the politicization of aid and the manipulation of humanitarian operations for political ends pose additional obstacles. Despite these challenges, the international community's commitment to humanitarian assistance remains paramount, emphasizing the need to alleviate the suffering of affected communities and pave the way for lasting peace.

4. Monitoring and Observer Missions:

Monitoring and observer missions established by the international community play a crucial role in contributing to the resolution of the Israeli-Palestinian conflict. These missions comprise representatives from various countries, international organizations, and non governmental organizations who closely monitor the situation on the ground. They document human rights violations, acts of violence, and any breaches of international law, ensuring that relevant parties are held accountable for their actions.

The presence of monitoring and observer missions acts as a deterrence mechanism, discouraging potential escalations and contributing to conflict de-escalation. By reporting on violations and breaches, these missions provide valuable information to the international community, enabling diplomatic and policy decisions to be based on accurate and up-to-date assessments of the situation. Furthermore, monitoring missions can facilitate confidence-building measures, such as overseeing ceasefires, troop withdrawals, and the implementation of agreed-upon frameworks.

However, the effectiveness of monitoring and observer missions can be limited by challenges such as restricted access to certain areas, threats to the safety of mission members, and non-cooperation from the parties involved. Nevertheless, the presence of these missions demonstrates the international community's commitment to transparency, accountability, and the adherence to international law, ultimately contributing to the pursuit of a just and sustainable resolution.

5. Economic Investment and Development:

Economic development and investment have the potential to play a transformative role in
resolving the Israeli-Palestinian conflict. The international community recognizes this and has sought to support economic initiatives that foster cooperation, job creation, and sustainable growth in the region. By promoting economic interdependence and shared prosperity, international actors can contribute to the stabilization of the conflict and create incentives for peaceful coexistence.

Economic initiatives often include joint industrial zones, cross-border infrastructure projects, and international trade agreements. These projects aim to integrate the economies of Israel and Palestine, encouraging collaboration and mutual dependencies. They facilitate increased economic exchanges, create employment opportunities, promote entrepreneurship, and enhance living standards for both Israeli and Palestinian populations.

However, economic development initiatives face challenges such as disparities in resources, access to markets, and limitations imposed by the conflict, which impede the full realization of their potential. The political environment, the settlement issue, and restrictions on freedom of movement also pose significant obstacles. Nevertheless, the international community's continued commitment to economic investment and development serves as a catalyst for conflict transformation, fostering socio-economic progress and providing tangible benefits to all stakeholders.

6. Advocacy and Public Opinion:

Public opinion plays a crucial role in shaping the Israeli-Palestinian conflict, and the international community has been actively involved in advocating for a just and peaceful resolution. Through advocacy efforts, countries, international organizations, and civil society groups raise awareness about the complexities, historical context, and consequences of the conflict. They aim to foster a broader understanding among the general public, policymakers, and opinion leaders, thereby influencing decision-making processes and encouraging support for peaceful solutions.

Advocacy efforts take various forms, such as public campaigns, media engagement, educational programs, and cultural exchanges campaigns. These initiatives aim to humanize the conflict, promote empathy, and challenge ingrained narratives that perpetuate hostility and division. By showcasing the shared values and aspirations of Israelis and Palestinians, advocacy efforts contribute to building bridges, fostering dialogue, and promoting a more nuanced understanding of the conflict.

Furthermore, advocacy for a just and peaceful resolution is not limited to public awareness campaigns. The international community also utilizes diplomatic channels, bilateral engagements, and international forums to advance their positions. These efforts include
drafting and sponsoring resolutions at the United Nations, participating in multilateral peace conferences, and engaging in bilateral negotiations with the parties involved. Through these platforms, the international community amplifies the voices of Israelis and Palestinians advocating for peace and encourages the adoption of measures that support a just and lasting resolution.

However, advocacy efforts face challenges in influencing public opinion and policy outcomes. There are entrenched narratives and interests that perpetuate division and hostility, making it difficult to change perspectives. Moreover, the Israeli-Palestinian conflict has become a deeply polarizing issue, with passionate and divergent viewpoints. Despite these challenges, the international community's dedication to public advocacy contributes to shaping a more informed, empathetic, and supportive global public opinion towards a peaceful resolution.

Conclusion:

The Israeli-Palestinian conflict is a complex, protracted issue that requires the collective efforts of the international community for its resolution. Through diplomatic mediation, support for peace initiatives, humanitarian assistance, monitoring and observer missions, economic investment and development, and advocacy and public opinion, the international community plays an extensive role in facilitating dialogue, promoting understanding, and fostering an environment conducive to peaceful resolution.

While there are significant challenges in navigating the complexities of the conflict, the international community's commitment remains vital. By leveraging their diplomatic influence, financial resources, and expertise, international actors can address the root causes of the conflict, provide essential support to affected populations, and promote the principles of justice, reconciliation, and coexistence. Moreover, by advocating for a just and peaceful resolution, the international community can shape public opinion, influence policy decisions, and contribute to the realization of a sustainable future for Israelis and Palestinians alike.

Living Together: Why Israel And Palestine
Must Find A Way Forward

———

United Nations' Involvement: Successes and Failures

Introduction:

The involvement of the United Nations (UN) in the Israeli-Palestinian conflict has been a complex and multifaceted endeavor. The UN, with its mandate to maintain international peace and security, has played a significant role in facilitating dialogue, promoting negotiations, and providing humanitarian aid in the region. This chapter delves deeper into the successes and failures of the UN's involvement in the Israeli-Palestinian conflict, shedding light on the challenges faced and exploring the nuanced dynamics at play.

Successes:

The successes of the United Nations in the Israeli-Palestinian conflict have been hard-won and have influenced the trajectory of peace efforts in the region. One of the most notable accomplishments was the adoption of UN General Assembly Resolution 181 in November 1947. This resolution, commonly known as the Partition Plan, proposed the establishment of separate Jewish and Arab states in Palestine. While the plan faced opposition and did not achieve its intended outcome, it remains a landmark expression of international support for self-determination and recognition of the rights and aspirations of both Jews and Arabs in the region.

Another significant contribution has been the UN's sustained efforts in providing humanitarian assistance to Palestinians affected by the conflict. The United Nations Relief and Works Agency for Palestine Refugees in the Near East (UNRWA) has been instrumental in supporting millions of Palestinian refugees, providing access to education, healthcare, and social services. Despite various challenges and criticisms, UNRWA has been crucial in addressing the needs of vulnerable populations and preventing further human suffering.

Additionally, the UN has played a vital role in facilitating peace processes and negotiations between Israel and the Palestinians. The Camp David Accords of 1978, brokered by the UN Secretary-General, led to an Israel-Egypt peace treaty. This significant breakthrough normalized relations between Israel and an Arab state and set a precedent for future diplomatic endeavors. Notably, the Oslo Accords, facilitated with UN assistance in the 1990s, established a framework for bilateral negotiations and outlined principles for a peaceful resolution. While the accords faced setbacks and unresolved issues, they marked a significant milestone in the pursuit of lasting peace.

Failures:
Despite its successes, the United Nations' involvement in the Israeli-Palestinian conflict has also encountered failures, highlighting the complexities and entrenched nature of the conflict. One of the primary challenges has been the difficulty in enforcing Security Council resolutions related to the conflict effectively. Although the Security Council has adopted numerous resolutions, ranging from calls for a ceasefire to demands for the end of settlement activities, their implementation has often been obstructed or ignored by the parties involved. The absence of stronger enforcement mechanisms and greater international consensus has lessened the impact and efficacy of these resolutions, raising questions about the UN's ability to ensure compliance with international law.

Furthermore, the politicization of the Israeli-Palestinian conflict within the UN system has significantly hindered progress. The disproportionate attention given to this issue, often resulting in biased resolutions and excessive criticism of Israel, has eroded trust between the parties involved. The perceived bias has undermined the UN's role as an impartial mediator, hindering genuine dialogue and obstructing efforts towards a comprehensive and equitable solution. It is crucial for the UN to uphold its principles of impartiality and ensure that all parties are held accountable for their actions and commitments.

Another area of failure has been the UN's peacekeeping efforts in the region. The United Nations Interim Force in Lebanon (UNIFIL), established in 1978, has faced criticism for its limited ability to prevent conflict escalation and address cross-border attacks. The complexities of the Israeli-Palestinian conflict, with intertwined political, historical, and religious dimensions, have presented significant hurdles for peacekeeping operations and conflict resolution efforts. The UN's inability to prevent the outbreak of violence during various outbreaks, such as the Second Intifada, has raised questions about its effectiveness in maintaining peace and stability in the region.

Conclusion:

The United Nations' involvement in the Israeli-Palestinian conflict has been both influential and challenging. Despite the failures encountered along the way, achievements such as the Partition Plan, humanitarian assistance through UNRWA, and peace negotiation facilitation have left lasting imprints on the region's trajectory. However, the challenges faced by the UN in this conflict necessitate constant evaluation, introspection, and reforms. Striving for greater impartiality, stronger enforcement mechanisms, and a more comprehensive approach are crucial to overcoming systemic obstacles and building a path towards a just and lasting peace. The UN must continue to engage all

parties involved, encourage mutual
recognition, and foster an environment conducive to
sustainable peace in the Israeli Palestinian conflict.

Living Together: Why Israel And Palestine
Must Find A Way Forward

Regional Actors: Influence and Initiatives for Peace

Introduction:

In the Israeli-Palestinian conflict, regional actors play a significant and complex role in shaping the dynamics and outcomes of peace initiatives. Their involvement and influence have the potential to either contribute to positive change or exacerbate tensions. This chapter delves deeper into the impact and complexity of regional actors' engagement, highlighting their initiatives, challenges, and potential for constructive contributions to the peace process.

The Role of Regional Actors:

Regional actors, comprising neighboring countries and influential regional powers, have multifaceted interests and motivations in the resolution of the Israeli-Palestinian conflict. They recognize that the ongoing conflict poses significant challenges to regional stability, hampers economic development, and fuels extremism. Additionally, the status quo undermines diplomatic relations and cooperation between neighboring states and societies. Thus, regional actors are driven by a combination of pragmatic and idealistic factors to engage in peace initiatives.

Egypt's Historic Mediation Efforts:

Egypt, as a key regional actor, has a rich history of involvement in Israeli-Palestinian peace initiatives. Building on the success of the Camp David Accords in 1978, Egypt has consistently played an active and influential role in mediating fragile ceasefires and facilitating dialogue between the conflicting parties. Its geographical proximity to both Israel and the Palestinian territories gives Egypt a unique position to bridge divides and promote understanding.

Over the years, Egypt's mediation efforts have focused on achieving a sustainable two state solution that respects the rights and aspirations of both Israelis and Palestinians. Through shuttle diplomacy, hosting bilateral and multilateral meetings, and leveraging its historical ties, Egypt has successfully brokered several critical agreements. For example, it facilitated the 2012 ceasefire agreement between Israel and Hamas, which temporarily brought quiet to the conflict-torn Gaza Strip. These commendable achievements demonstrate the potential of regional actors to serve as catalysts for positive change by providing a neutral platform for negotiations and leveraging their diplomatic influence.

Jordan's Strategic Role in Peacebuilding:

Jordan, as a neighboring country to both Israel and the Palestinian territories, holds a strategic position in the conflict. With historical ties to the Palestinian cause and a keen interest in regional stability, Jordan has consistently worked towards peacebuilding efforts. As the custodian of Muslim and Christian holy sites in Jerusalem, Jordan bears a unique responsibility to protect the religious and cultural heritage of the region, granting it moral standing in peace negotiations.

Under the leadership of King Abdullah II, Jordan has been actively engaged in promoting peace and dialogue between Israeli and Palestinian leaders. The country's commitment to the two-state solution and its active participation in multilateral forums, such as the Arab League, provide a platform for constructive discussions and initiatives. Jordan's peacebuilding efforts extend beyond diplomatic channels, with initiatives such as Track II diplomacy and projects that encourage people-to-people interactions. These initiatives aim to build trust and understanding between communities, fostering an environment conducive to sustainable peace.

Saudi Arabia's Visionary Approach:

In recent years, Saudi Arabia has put forth its own peace initiative, known as the Arab Peace Initiative. Originally proposed in 2002 and reconfirmed in 2007 and 2017, this comprehensive framework seeks to resolve the Israeli-Palestinian conflict through Arab recognition of Israel and an end to the occupation. In return, Arab states expect the establishment of an independent Palestinian state with East Jerusalem as its capital, and a just solution to the refugee issue.

The Arab Peace Initiative outlines a visionary roadmap for a comprehensive and just peace settlement, focusing on the Arab world's commitment to regional stability and the resolution of the Israeli-Palestinian conflict. By presenting a unified regional approach, Saudi Arabia exemplifies the potential of regional actors to contribute innovative ideas and suggestions that could pave the way for a just and lasting peace agreement.

Challenges and Opportunities:
While regional actors bring significant potential for positive contributions, their involvement in the Israeli-Palestinian conflict is not without challenges. Divisions and divergent national interests among regional actors often impede cohesive action. Historical grievances, power struggles, and differing priorities related to security and regional influence frequently overshadow collective efforts.

Moreover, the complex dynamics between Israel and Iran, as well as tensions within the Arab world, pose significant challenges to regional actors' ability to effectively engage in peace initiatives. The Iranian-Israeli rivalry and geopolitical competition further complicate the efforts of regional actors, as they often seek to exploit the conflict for their own interests.

However, despite these considerable obstacles, regional actors possess the agency to leverage their influence, cultivate alliances, and engage in sustained dialogue to overcome challenges and work towards a shared vision of peace. The changing dynamics in the region, such as the recent normalization agreements between Israel and some Arab states, offer opportunities for increased cooperation and collective efforts towards a comprehensive peace settlement.

Conclusion:

Regional actors wield substantial influence in the Israeli-Palestinian conflict, and their involvement can decisively shape the trajectory of peace efforts. By leveraging their diplomatic channels, strategic positions, and regional alliances, regional actors can play a crucial role in encouraging dialogue, fostering cooperation, and pushing for a just resolution.

It is essential for regional actors to maintain their engagement, despite the challenges they encounter. Constructive contributions from regional actors, aligned with international support, offer hope for a future where Israelis and Palestinians can coexist in peace and security. Through sustained dialogue, mediation, and an unwavering commitment to a two state solution, regional actors can collectively work towards a comprehensive, just, and lasting peace settlement in the region.

Living Together: Why Israel And Palestine
Must Find A Way Forward

Conclusion:

The Importance of Finding a Way Forward and the Potential Benefits of Coexistence.

The Israeli-Palestinian conflict, an ongoing struggle marked by deep historical, political, and religious complexities, has been a topic of great debate and contention for decades. The land of Israel and Palestine holds deep significance for both Israelis and Palestinians, making it a highly contested territory with conflicting claims and narratives. The repercussions of this conflict have been felt not only by the people directly involved but also by the broader international community, which has grappled with the consequences of a seemingly unsolvable problem.

Throughout this narrative, it becomes evident that the Israeli-Palestinian conflict is deeply rooted in a complex web of historical grievances, competing national aspirations, and ongoing violence. Both Israelis and Palestinians have experienced immense pain, loss, and suffering as a result of this conflict. The narratives held by each side have often been at odds with each other, reinforcing a cycle of mistrust and hostility. However, it is crucial to recognize that there is no inherent incompatibility between Israelis and Palestinians. Both groups share an undeniable connection to the land they call home and have legitimate claims to it.

The Israeli perspective is shaped by historical experiences of persecution, antisemitism, and the need for a homeland where Jews can feel safe and secure. The establishment of the modern State of Israel in 1948 was seen as the realization of the Jewish people's longing for self-determination after a long history of exile and discrimination. Similarly, Palestinians view their struggle as one for self-determination and the right to their homeland. For them, the displacement caused by the establishment of Israel in 1948, known as the Nakba (catastrophe), remains a deeply rooted and ongoing grievance.

Despite the challenges, it is essential for all parties involved to consider the profound benefits that coexistence and peace could bring. A just and durable peace agreement would not only allow Israelis and Palestinians to live side by side in security and dignity, but it would also provide stability to the region as a whole. The potential for economic growth, cultural exchange, and political cooperation between the two nations is immense and should not be underestimated.

Coexistence between Israelis and Palestinians would create a symbiotic relationship that draws upon the strength and diversity of both societies. It would foster innovation, leading to joint initiatives in fields such as technology, agriculture, healthcare, and renewable energy. By pooling resources, expertise, and knowledge, Israelis and Palestinians could spur economic development and improve the quality of life for both peoples. Moreover, an end to the conflict would facilitate the creation of networks, collaborations, and partnerships that would benefit not only the two nations but also the wider region.

Economically, peace would pave the way for increased trade and investment opportunities. The Palestinian territories, with their educated and talented population, offer immense potential for growth and development. The implementation of peace agreements, accompanied by support from the international community, could bring about a transformative economic boom in the region. Israelis and Palestinians, working together, could harness their collective skills and resources to build a prosperous future for themselves, offering a model of success that could inspire other regions facing conflicts.

In addition to economic prosperity, coexistence would offer opportunities for cultural exchange and the preservation of shared heritage. Israelis and Palestinians have a rich history that intertwines their cultures, religions, and traditions. Embracing coexistence would allow for the celebration and exploration of their shared roots, fostering greater understanding, empathy, and respect. This cultural exchange would contribute to a broader narrative of peace, challenging the entrenched narratives of conflict and division. Through initiatives such as joint festivals, art exhibitions, and educational programs, Israelis and Palestinians could foster deeper connections and appreciate each other's unique contributions.

Furthermore, peace between Israelis and Palestinians would have significant implications on an international scale. The Israeli-Palestinian conflict has long been used as a rallying point for extremists and a source of regional destabilization. A resolution would weaken the appeal used by radical groups to recruit followers and diminish the threat of terrorism both in the region and globally. Stability in this volatile part of the world would have positive ripple effects, creating opportunities for cross-border collaboration, economic integration, and regional cooperation on shared challenges such as water scarcity, climate change, and security.

Finding a way forward is a complex and arduous task that demands the genuine commitment of all sides. It requires courageous leadership willing to take risks and make difficult compromises for the betterment of their people. Above all, it necessitates a paradigm shift in thinking, where grievances are acknowledged but not allowed to perpetuate a cycle of retribution. A constructive and inclusive dialogue, where all voices are heard, grievances are aired, and empathy is nurtured, is vital in creating a shared vision for a future based on peace, justice, and coexistence.

In the pursuit of a resolution, the international community plays a critical role. UN resolutions, diplomatic efforts, economic support, and security assurances can all contribute to building trust and facilitating a just and lasting resolution. Regional actors, neighboring countries, and international organizations should work collaboratively to encourage dialogues and initiatives that promote reconciliation and peace. By providing political, economic, and logistical support, the international community can help create an environment conducive to constructive negotiations and foster an atmosphere of trust and mutual understanding.

Education and grassroots initiatives also have a crucial role to play in cultivating a culture of peace and coexistence among the younger generations. By introducing curricula that foster empathy, promote critical thinking, and encourage dialogue, both Israeli and Palestinian children could learn about each other's history, culture, and aspirations in a more balanced and nuanced manner. Exchanges and joint programs that bring young Israelis and Palestinians together offer a powerful platform to humanize the "other" and build lasting friendships based on mutual respect.

In conclusion, the Israeli-Palestinian conflict is a complex and challenging issue that requires a deep examination of its historical roots and a thoughtful approach to finding a way forward. The potential benefits of coexistence and a peaceful resolution are profound and far-reaching. By recognizing the shared humanity of Israelis and Palestinians and embracing the core values of peace, justice, and reconciliation, we can move towards a future where both nations can flourish together. The time has come for all stakeholders involved to transcend barriers of mistrust, break the cycle of violence, and embark on a path towards a better future for all.

<h1 style="text-align:center">About The Author</h1>

Alexandre-Luc Wahlström Smith

Starting as an architectural photographer in London, Alexandre travelled the world, absorbing and documenting the beauty of the world's greatest buildings.

During his down time Alexandre studied psychology and other social sciences doing courses at Yale, Berkeley California. Alexandre-luc then went on to study economics and international relations and conflict resolution and Gothenburg University in Sweden.

He is also happily married to an anthropology doctor, who shares his love for exploring and understanding the world. Together, they have two children who bring joy and excitement to their lives.

Napoleon: A Comprehensive Biography Of A Military And Political Genius Napoleon:

A Comprehensive Biography of a Military and Political Genius" is a thought-provoking book that provides a comprehensive and balanced view of Napoleon's life and achievements. The book covers Napoleon's early years, military and political genius, constructive rule, and civic innovations. It challenges the stereotypes of Napoleon as a figure to be reviled and provides insights into his psychology and power of regimental pride. The book also examines the impact of Napoleon's achievements and evaluates his legacy. This engaging narrative style book is a must-read for anyone interested in history, military tactics, and leadership.

Living In A Postcolonial World: Voices Of Marginalised Communities

This book provides a comprehensive overview of postcolonial literature, examining its key themes, theories, and methodologies. It explores the experiences and perspectives of marginalized voices from former colonies, challenging the dominant narratives constructed by colonial powers. The book highlights the power dynamics and stereotypes perpetuated by colonialist literature and calls for a reinterpretation of history and culture from the perspective of the colonized. It also explores the concept of hybridity and diaspora, providing a more inclusive and nuanced understanding of the complexities of postcolonial societies.

Niccolò Machiavelli: The Life And Legacy Of A Renaissance Philosopher And Political Theorist

Niccolò Machiavelli: The Life and Legacy of a Renaissance Philosopher and Political Theorist" is a book that delves into the life and ideas of one of the most influential thinkers of the Italian Renaissance. This book provides a comprehensive overview of Machiavelli's life, his political ideas, and his impact on modern political philosophy. It is a must-read for anyone interested in the history of political thought and the development of modern political theory.